After Emmaus

After Emmaus

Biblical Models
for the New Evangelization

Marcel Dumais

LITURGICAL PRESS
Collegeville, Minnesota

www.litpress.org

1   2   3   4   5   6   7   8   9

Library of Congress Cataloging-in-Publication Data

Dumais, Marcel, 1936–
    After Emmaus : biblical models for the new evangelization / Marcel Dumais.
        pages cm
    ISBN 978-0-8146-3761-6 — ISBN 978-0-8146-3786-9 (ebook)
    1. Evangelistic work—Catholic Church.   I. Title.
BX2347.4.D86   2014
266'.2—dc23   2014008294

Contents

Introduction   1

Chapter 1
Why a New Evangelization?   5

Chapter 2
Direct Proclamation of the Gospel
(The Kerygmatic Model)   19

Chapter 3
The Athens Model   37

Chapter 4
The Evangelical Model of Humanism, Part One
Jesus: A Man of Compassion   58

Chapter 5
The Evangelical Model of Humanism, Part Two
The Way to Happiness   79

Chapter 6
The Model of Emmaus   92

Conclusion   110

Notes   119

Introduction

The question of a "new evangelization" is at the heart of the current concerns of the Catholic Church. This raises a first question, what does it mean to attach the adjective "new" to the noun "evangelization?" After all, in the life of the church since the Second Vatican Council, evangelization has been presented as constituting the essential mission of the church. This is what we read particularly in the two major pontifical texts on mission published since the council: Paul VI's apostolic exhortation on evangelization in the modern world, *Evangelii Nuntiandi* (1975), and John Paul II's encyclical on the missionary mandate, *Redemptoris Missio* (1990).[1]

At the moment when the Vatican announced and began preparations for a synod of the universal church on the theme of "the new evangelization," which took place in October 2012, there appeared the apostolic exhortation of the preceding synod of the church, which had taken place in October 2008 on the theme of "The Word of God in the Life and Mission of the Church."[2] The title of that exhortation underlines the strong link between the Bible and evangelization. The third part of the document bears the title *Verbum pro Mundo* (The Word for the World).

Bible and evangelization—this subject has been a personal concern of mine for the past forty years, ever since the time I spent preparing my doctoral dissertation on the missionary discourses in the Acts of the Apostles, which was published under the title *Le langage de l'évangélisation* (The Language of Evangelization).[3] Since that time, courses, research projects, publications, conferences, and retreats in different parts of the

1

world have brought me back to this theme from various points of view.[4] The current situation of the church, and especially the convocation of a Synod on the new evangelization, call me to take up once again the question of the Bible and mission from a new perspective. It is my intention to contribute to reflection on this question and to the initiatives called for by the contemporary situation.

The new evangelization is an "opportunity," or more properly a "grace," for the church. It is necessary because the church cannot be satisfied with structural reforms of the institution or with reflection on and public statements about moral questions. It must first of all focus on what is strictly speaking "theological," on what constitutes the purpose of its existence and its mission, that is, the question of Jesus Christ and of the God of Jesus Christ, the question of faith, hope, and love. In concentrating on these questions, the new evangelization comes back to what is most profound in human beings: their reason for living, that which gives them the possibility of living their humanity in its fullness.

In order to be faithful to our mission today, we must continually return to the New Testament and adapt the essential content of the witness of Jesus and the apostles to our own times. A survey of the biblical material reveals that Jesus and the apostles used various approaches in bearing witness, depending on the context and the times; these approaches are models for us and serve as fundamental reference points.

The present work is intended to be an accessible reference for all disciples of Jesus Christ who are deeply concerned with the present situation of the Christian faith and the future of the mission of Jesus Christ in our world. It is meant to be a serious work, based on sound research, but with a minimum of technical apparatus. In the presentation of certain Scripture passages, references will provide an opportunity to undertake more extensive analysis of texts and delve into the reasoning process that leads to the proposed interpretations. My wish is to open some directions for a personal reading of the Scriptures from the point of view of evangelization. The biblical models chosen do not pretend to be exhaustive. Even the presentation of each model is not exhaustive.

The first chapter will raise the question of the new evangelization and its purpose. We will attempt to clarify how the new situation of Christianity in our Western secularized world pushes us to transform our traditional ways of defining the content, the agents, and the approaches to evangelization. The five following chapters will treat biblical models that we can consider as our first points of reference for the task of evangelization today. More precisely, two chapters will be dedicated to the work of evangelization carried out by the apostles, and the other three chapters will look at the evangelizing that Jesus did. The source text for the first two chapters will be the Acts of the Apostles, which is the book of the mission of the first witnesses commissioned by Jesus. Obviously, the gospels will be our reference point for the mission of Jesus.

If there is something original in this project, it is perhaps the way of looking at the biblical texts presenting the mission of Jesus and the apostles. These texts not only provide the content of evangelization, but they also serve as models of how to approach the task of evangelizing, models that the disciples of Jesus are called to take as their inspiration for their mission in the world, or rather, in the worlds we live in today. This approach to the texts of the Bible may be surprising at first. We have become used to considering the Bible from the perspective of the content of our faith (truths to believe, precepts to observe), but very little from the point of view of models of evangelization and of faith. The narrative approach to the biblical texts teaches us to look at the gospels and the Acts of the Apostles for what they were first of all, stories about events.

The biblical models are called to be realized in all cultural and social contexts. The present work is written in the view of evangelization in the secularized world that is mine.

I would add a note regarding my writing style. I want to enter into a dialogue with readers who are personally interested in the new evangelization. The presentation of each biblical model will include or be followed by reflections, and sometimes with questions that are intended to invite the reader to pursue his or her own reflection on the relevance and on the ways of using that model in his or her own context.

Chapter 1

Why a New Evangelization?

On September 21, 2010, Pope Benedict XVI established a Pontifical Council for the Promotion of the New Evangelization.[1] Shortly thereafter he announced that the next Synod of Bishops, scheduled for October 2012, would treat "The New Evangelization for the Transmission of the Christian Faith." The *Lineamenta* for this synod appeared in February 2011; this document served as an instrument of consultation directed to the bishops in order to prepare what is called the *Instrumentum Laboris*—the working document that the participants at the synod were to have at hand.

The expression "new evangelization," however, is not new. Since the beginning of his pontificate, Pope Benedict XVI had spoken frequently in his discourses and homilies about the need of a new evangelization for the church. In the apostolic letter in which he created the new Pontifical Council, the pope said that the evangelizing mission of the church today "has been particularly challenged by an abandonment of the faith—a phenomenon progressively more manifest in societies and cultures that for centuries seemed to be permeated by the Gospel."[2] An example of this abandonment of the faith is found in the European Parliament's refusal to recognize in its charter the "Christian roots of Europe," an affirmation requested by the Vatican and certain European countries. On a larger scale, it is more and more difficult to define the West—i.e., the countries of Western Europe and North America—as Christian countries. These countries, which were evangelized long ago, are in need of a "new evangelization," that is, a new proclamation of Jesus Christ and of the Gospel.[3]

The consciousness of a need for a new evangelization emerged gradually in the church long before the arrival of Pope Benedict. The Second Vatican Council treated as one of its central themes the question of the relationship between the church and the contemporary world, and this gave birth to the beautiful document *Gaudium et Spes* (Pastoral Constitution on the Church in the Modern World). In addition, the conciliar decree *Ad Gentes* (On the Mission Activity of the Church) recognized that profound transformations in our societies can call for a new kind of missionary activity (*Ad Gentes* 6). In 1975 Pope Paul VI published a magnificent apostolic exhortation, *Evangelii Nuntiandi* (Evangelization in the Modern World), in which he wrote that evangelization is even more necessary "as a result of the frequent situations of dechristianization in our day; it also proves equally necessary for innumerable people who have been baptized but who live quite outside Christian life, for simple people who have a certain faith but an imperfect knowledge of the foundations of that faith, for intellectuals who feel the need to know Jesus Christ in a light different from the instruction they received as children, and for many others" (*Evangelii Nuntiandi* 52). Thinking of those who have distanced themselves from the church, he added, "the Church's evangelizing action . . . must constantly seek the proper means and language for presenting, or re-presenting, to them God's revelation and faith in Jesus Christ" (*Evangelii Nuntiandi* 56).[4] The church consists of those who believe in Jesus Christ. In other words, those who have been evangelized must in their turn become evangelizers in their human environment.

Pope John Paul II is credited with creating the expression "new evangelization," which he used in a homily preached in Poland in 1979.[5] He used this expression again on many occasions thereafter, and in 2001, in his apostolic letter, *Novo millennio ineunte* (At the Beginning of the New Millennium), he proposed it as the mission for the church in the third millennium of its history. We might mention in particular the formula he used at Port-au-Prince, Haiti, at the opening session of the plenary assembly of CELAM (the Latin American Episcopal Conference): "a commitment . . . to a new evangelization. New in its ardor, in its methods, in its expression." Later on John Paul II would come back several times to these three dimensions of the novelty of this evangelization. From 1985 onwards, Pope John Paul, and later Benedict XVI, would clearly apply the expression "new evangelization" to the situation of a dechristianized Europe.[6]

If the concept of new evangelization has its roots in the dechristianizing of many Western countries, the synod of the universal church in October 2012 treated the situation of the church not only in Europe or North America. The discussions considered the diverse ways in which the project could be applied to different continents. For example, Pope Benedict XVI, in the post-synodal exhortation *Africae Munus*, which he presented during his voyage to Benin on November 19, 2011, incorporated a section on "The New Evangelization." He presented it as "an urgent task for Christians in Africa because they too need to reawaken their enthusiasm for being members of the Church. Guided by the Spirit of the risen Lord, they are called to live the Good News as individuals, in their families and in society, and to proclaim it with fresh zeal to persons near and far, using the new methods that divine Providence has placed at our disposal for its spread."[7]

However, the present work is concerned primarily with the evangelization of the secularized West. Thus we will be reflecting on the use of biblical models of mission for the situation of the church in secularized settings. I remain convinced, nonetheless, that the biblical models presented are fundamental for evangelization in every region of the world and in any situation of the church.

In the apostolic exhortation *Verbum Domini*, which appeared on September 30, 2010, following the Synod of Bishops on The Word of God in the Life and Mission of the Church, Pope Benedict writes:

> Our own time, then, must be increasingly marked by a new hearing of God's word and a new evangelization. Recovering the centrality of the divine word in the Christian life leads us to appreciate anew the deepest meaning of the forceful appeal of Pope John Paul II: to pursue the *missio ad gentes* and vigorously to embark upon the new evangelization, especially in those nations where the Gospel has been forgotten or meets with indifference as a result of widespread secularity. (*Verbum Domini* 122)

In addition, we have to say, in the present circumstances, that the situation of a growing majority of people in the West is not unlike that of people in the Southern Hemisphere: they have not even heard a proclamation of the Gospel! In both cases, what we are often dealing with is a mission *ad gentes*, a first evangelization! The principal difference between the two worlds resides rather in the attitude people have toward religion: while the people of the Southern Hemisphere remain largely "religious," those of the North are powerfully marked by what is called "secularization."

The New Evangelization in a Secularized World

In fact we have passed from a religious world into a secularized world. Already in 1988, in his post-synodal apostolic exhortation *Christifideles laici* (The Vocation and Mission of the Lay Faithful), Pope John Paul II spoke of the "urgency" of a new evangelization involving the laity, and he indicated why this is so: "the phenomenon of de-Christianization . . . strikes long-standing Christian people and . . . continually calls for a re-evangelization" (*Christifideles laici* 4).

It is widely acknowledged that the society and culture of the countries of Western Europe and North America have become increasingly secularized. Pope Benedict XVI often spoke of this reality in his addresses. I cite an extract from one of his discourses that will allow us to clarify the meaning of secularization. Speaking to a group of German bishops on November 10, 2006, he stated that the Federal Republic of Germany "shares the western world's situation of a culture characterized by secularization, in which God tends more and more to disappear from the public consciousness."[8] In his public addresses, Benedict XVI often juxtaposed the terms "secularization" and "eclipse of the sense of God."[9]

The principal reason for the dechristianizing of the Western world is the secularization of our societies. This reality is complex in its causes and in its components. For our purposes, I would first of all say the following: a secularized world is a world whose culture and society are no longer religious . . . that is to say no longer Christian and that seems to be the case for a growing number of Western countries. For example, we can safely say that in France and Quebec people are no longer living in a Catholic society and culture.

A secularized society is a society that is not open to the transcendent, to God. It is a society where the option for the transcendent, for God, becomes a question of choice.[10] Religion is pushed into the sphere of private choices. Thus, why believe in God? Why choose, in particular, to believe in Jesus Christ? This choice is not self-evident among the broad range of beliefs currently presented to us.

One of the characteristics of a secular society, in effect, is pluralism. A number of factors lead to secularity. It is not simply a result of the development of the consumer society. First of all, it is caused by advances in the sciences and in technology, by the flow of information through the media, and by the fact that pluralism has taken root. There is a plurality of views concerning the world, society, and religion. This in turn leads to leaving freedom of choice to individuals. To become a Christian is a choice, a personal option. It is no longer an integral component of belonging to a particular society or a particular nation.

Thus, in Quebec, Catholicism has gradually become a minority religion under the effects of pluralism, even if a good number of people marked by secularism still continue to have their children baptized because they have some vague belief in God and the Catholic Church is their convenient point of reference.

To illustrate the steady social decline of the "Catholic" character of a certain number of societies in the West, I cite the case of France and will present the results of a very important recent study published in 2007.[11] Here are some statistics from this inquiry: only one out of two French citizens (51 percent) identify themselves as "Catholic" (in 1994, 67 percent did); only 52 percent of those who declare that they are Catholic consider the existence of God "certain" or "probable"; and a minority of those Catholics (18 percent) believe in a "personal God with whom they can have a relationship,"[12] a belief that is at the heart of the Christian faith. Nonetheless, if there are fewer and fewer "cradle Catholics," there is a significant number of "adult converts." In 2006 there were approximately 10,000 catechumens, most of them between the ages of 25 and 40.

More recently, a poll taken in January 2011 revealed that 34 percent of French citizens say that they are "atheists" and 36 percent claim to be believers. Of the remaining 30 percent, 22 percent of those polled "do not know if they believe in God but do pose the question," while 8 percent "do not know, and do not even pose the question."[13] This poll reveals, however, that 5 percent of those who "affirm that they do not practice any religion, do nonetheless believe in God" and that 34 percent of those answering the survey "call themselves Catholics, but admit that they do not believe in God."[14] The boundaries between believers and nonbelievers are, therefore, not so clear.

These polls are revealing, but they should be viewed with some reservations, for the terms used, such as "atheist," are not defined. Danièle Hervieu-Léger, a preeminent sociologist of religions, has come to the conclusion that the various recent surveys reveal the triumph of "indifferentism" more than atheism. By that she understands an indifference vis-à-vis doctrines and religious practices, reflecting a society that lives within an inner worldly horizon that emphasizes self-construction and individualism. People live as if God did not exist. If someone is a believer and religious, it is by choice.

If we want to understand how, in the course of history, we gradually arrived in a secularized world, the best account by far is the superb recent work of Charles Taylor, entitled *A Secular Age*.[15] In the introduction to this extraordinary tome Taylor offers three meanings of secularity and favors the third one that "would focus on the conditions of belief": the passage "from a society where belief in God is unchallenged and indeed, unproblematic, to one in which it is understood to be one option among others, and frequently not the easiest to embrace. In this meaning . . . at least many milieux in the United States are secularized, and I would argue that the United States as a whole is. Clear contrast cases today would be the majority of Muslim societies."[16]

I would introduce here a concept that Charles Taylor does not use, but that is widespread in Europe and especially in France: the notion of *laïcité* ("laicism"). *Laïcité* is the separation of roles and powers of the church from those of the state. There is a positive sense of the term when this separation of church and state is seen with an attitude of mutual respect, and even support, for the role and objectives of the other, together with recognition of religious liberty. This seems to be the case, for example, in the United States, in Canada, and in several European countries. We have seen above, however, that secularized society and culture do not include openness to the transcendent, to God.

According to several authors, the United States is in some ways an exception with regard to secularization, for the religious dimension is still an integral part of the society and culture of the majority of its citizens. Surveys similar to those cited above contrast significantly with the statistics in France: 90 percent of Americans say they believe in God; 70 percent of them say that they pray or are members of a religious community.[17] According to another study, 92 percent of Americans believe in God and more than a third go to church at least once a week.[18] In an address delivered to the cardinals during the consistory of February 2012, then-Cardinal-designate Timothy Dolan, archbishop of New York, said: "New York—without denying its dramatic evidence of graphic secularism—is also a very religious city."[19] In Canada, Quebec is the most secularized society.[20]

Nonetheless, we should note the following: if there is less and less interest for what is "religious" (the religions) in our societies, there is a variety of expressions of a quest for the "spiritual." Many of our contemporaries who have abandoned all forms of religious practice feel a "void" and they have a desire to put a spiritual dimension back into their lives. We will discuss this phenomenon in the third chapter.

We should also make a distinction between "secularity" and "secularism." Secularism is the option, on the part of individuals or groups, to deny the existence of the transcendent (God). The secular mentality does not as such exclude the existence of the transcendent, but the transcendent does not enter into their parameters to explain the world.

In a secularized world, what is at stake in the mission of evangelization is in the realm of theology rather than morality. In other words, it is concerned with the question of faith. It is in this perspective that the reflections on the different biblical models presented in the following chapters are developed.

The Church of the Future: Smaller Numbers?

Is the church called to be a minority in our world? At one point in the gospels, Jesus speaks of his disciples as "a little flock" with the mission of being "salt of the earth" and "light of the world" (Matt 5:13-16).

Cardinal Joseph Ratzinger, in his book *The Salt of the Earth,* which appeared in 1997, raised this question. Here are some extracts from his reflections:

> I had foreseen then [in 1970] . . . that the Church would become small, that one day she would become a Church comprising a minority of society and that she could then no longer continue with the large institutions and organizations that she has but would have to organize herself on a more modest scale. . . . The Church has to adjust herself gradually to a minority position, to another position in society.[21]

> It would be misguided, indeed, presumptuous, to design now a more or less finished model of the Church of tomorrow, which, more clearly than today, will be a Church of a minority.[22]

> Precisely an age in which Christianity is quantitatively reduced can bring this more conscious Christianity to a new vitality. In this sense it is indeed true that we are standing before a new kind of Christian era.[23]

> The Church must be aware of her quite specific mission: to be the world's escape from itself into the light of God and to keep open this possibility so that the air we breathe can penetrate the world.[24]

Will there be smaller numbers in the church of tomorrow? Certainly in the sense that more and more often people will be identified as "Christian" (Catholic, Orthodox, Protestant) not by virtue of being born into a family belonging to the Christian tradition, but by personally choosing to follow Jesus Christ and to be involved in the church. We must however beware of wanting to be a "church of the elite." Conversion to Jesus Christ and to the Gospel is always imperfect, always in need of renewal. The expressions of faith by people of very modest learning and those more learned should all be able to find their place in a rich diversity. We should remain modest in our projections of what the church of the future will be. God, working through the Spirit, will always be the most important agent, the master of the mission.

The growth of secularization in the social and cultural environment that has formed me has gradually made me want to concentrate on what is essential in my life of faith. I would make Pope Benedict's observation during the visit of the German bishops mentioned above my own: "Secularization is a 'providential challenge for the Church.'" I would add: is it not also, for us practicing Christians, an opportunity to center ourselves—or to re-center ourselves—on what constitutes the heart of our faith, and consequently, the heart of our mission?

Evangelization: The Responsibility of All Disciples

A superficial reading of the gospels and the Acts of the Apostles can give the impression that communicating the Gospel and awakening faith is the ministry that Jesus gave to the apostles he chose, and therefore, in our own context, to their successors, those who govern the church: bishops, priests, and some lay people who have been specially designated for this mission.

It is not so. All Christians are called to be witnesses, that is, missionaries in the world in which they live, witnesses of God, witnesses of the life given in Jesus Christ. The mission is not a ministry reserved to a few. All believers in Jesus Christ are called to be missionaries; each and every believer, in his or her own way, is called to bear witness to Jesus Christ and the rich and full life that is given in him.

With this perspective, let us look once again at the gospels and the Acts of the Apostles. First of all, the gospels offer us three points of reference:

1. During his earthly life, Jesus chose, among his disciples, twelve apostles and sent them on mission (Luke 9:1-6).

In the Gospel of Luke we read in the following chapter that Jesus "appointed seventy-two others whom he sent ahead of him in pairs to every town and place he intended to visit," and he gave them a missionary mandate (Luke 10:1). These seventy-two disciples were likely all those he had assembled up to that point or at least all those who were disposed to commit themselves seriously to follow him. Thus Jesus sent all his disciples on mission.

2. According to the Gospel of Matthew, Jesus addresses his first great discourse to all his disciples (5:1). After having proclaimed the Beatitudes, which is a message of happiness for all humanity, he addresses his disciples explicitly and speaks to them of their mission in the world: to be "salt of the earth" and "light of the world." And he goes on to say that it is by the witness of their "good works" that they will be salt and light for the world (Matt 5:13-14). This invitation to be salt that gives flavor to life and light that illuminates the night is addressed to all Christians today. It is to his disciples of today that Jesus says "Go, therefore, and make disciples of all nations . . ." (Matt 28:19).

3. The Gospel of Luke recounts the apparition of Jesus to the eleven gathered with the disciples who remained faithful to him (Luke 24:36).[25] Thus Jesus gives to all his disciples the mission to be witnesses and he promises to send the Spirit for this mission that he entrusts to them (Luke 24:46-49).

As for the Acts of the Apostles, the book dedicated to the mission, Luke reports the coming of the Spirit on the disciples so that they may be his witnesses, his missionaries. The account of Pentecost in chapter two begins with this phrase. "When the time for Pentecost was fulfilled, they were all in one place together." The text goes on to say that "they were all filled with the Holy Spirit." The "all" represents the eleven apostles gathered in the upper room, "together with some women, including Mary the mother of Jesus, and his brothers," or even the crowd of "about one hundred and twenty believers" mentioned in Acts 1:15.

The book of Acts also mentions that this presence of the Spirit of Pentecost makes witnesses of other disciples: for example, Stephen (Acts 6:10), Philip (Acts 8:30), Paul and Barnabas (Acts 13:2-4). Very early in the life of the church, the first Christian community is shaken by the imprisonment of Peter and John. After their liberation, all the members gather and feel the need to pray to God. They make the following petition: "enable your servants to proclaim your word with all boldness" (Acts 4:29). Then they experience a new Pentecost. "As they prayed, the place where they were gathered shook, and they were all filled with the Holy Spirit and continued to speak the word of God with boldness" (Acts 4:31). Throughout the Acts of the Apostles the same expression is used to characterize the way in which the first Christians spoke about Jesus—they testify "boldly."[26]

The model of the first church in the Acts of the Apostles communicates a clear teaching, which is that all those who become Christians receive the Spirit of Pentecost in order to bear witness to Jesus Christ and to the Gospel in the world. To be Christian is to be a witness, to be a missionary.[27] Let us add this testimony of Paul who writes to his Christian community: "Since, then, we have the same spirit of faith, according to what is written, 'I believed, therefore I spoke' we too believe and therefore speak" (2 Cor 4:13).

An observation about making it happen: retrieving a missionary spirit, the kind of fundamental evangelizing that Jesus wanted, entails consequences for the church, and first of all for the life of ecclesial communities. Parishes have to become missionary, which means that those responsible for them need to prepare parishioners to become missionaries within their own environment by bearing witness to their family members, to people in the communities where they live and work, to all those who have not yet been touched by the Gospel and who constitute the majority in our secularized societies.

An Evangelization Centered on Jesus Christ

Remember another event that we were invited to enter into along with the Synod on New Evangelization: a "Year of Faith," proclaimed by Pope Benedict XVI on October 11, 2011.[28] It began with the opening of the Synod on New Evangelization, precisely on October 11, 2012, to commemorate the fiftieth anniversary of the opening of the Second Vatican Council and ended on November 24, 2013, the feast of Christ the King. This Year of Faith, which is offered to all the faithful, is intended first of all to help Catholics come to a deeper understanding of "the foundation of the Christian faith," which is, in Pope Benedict's words, "the encounter with an event, a person, which gives life a new horizon and a decisive direction."[29]

The pope points out that

> The Year of Faith is intended to contribute to a renewed conversion to the Lord Jesus and to the rediscovery of the faith, so that all members of the church may be credible and joyful witnesses of the risen Lord in the world of today, capable of leading many people to the "door of faith." This "door" opens wide to manifest Jesus Christ, present in our midst "always . . . until the end of the age" (Matt 28:20). Jesus Christ shows us how the art of living is learned by an intense relationship with Him.
>
> Through his love, Jesus Christ attracts to himself the people of every generation; in every age he convokes the church, entrusting her with the proclamation of the Gospel by a mandate that is ever new. Today, too, there is a need for stronger ecclesial commitment to new evangelization in order to rediscover the joy of believing and the enthusiasm for communicating the faith.[30]

To sum up, all Christians are called to contribute to evangelization, that is, to bear witness to Jesus Christ in their milieu. What does it mean concretely for us, in our local church, to say that all disciples of the Lord are called to be missionaries, to witness to Jesus Christ in their environment? Is the time ripe for this idea? What means can we use in order to invite and help all Christians to be missionaries in their milieu? Do we need to modify our pastoral approach in order to accomplish this task?

The purpose of the following chapters is to examine how Jesus and the apostles were evangelizing witnesses in their milieu—and how to use their approaches in the world today—taking as our guide writings of the New Testament, and more specifically, the gospels and the Acts of the Apostles. We will refer occasionally to the letters that Paul addressed to his Christian communities, that is, to those already converted. Although the Pauline texts more properly concern catechesis or theological instruction, they do contain occasional reminders of his evangelizing mission to them.[31]

An evangelization centered on Jesus Christ does not necessarily imply a direct proclamation—far from it. It is interesting to examine the different biblical models of evangelization. In the chapters of this work, we are going to look at four great biblical models of mission. The four biblical models, the four approaches to evangelization that are presented and are intended to inspire us, are the following: (1) the kerygmatic model, (2) the model used at Athens, (3) the evangelical model of humanism, and (4) the model used in the story of Emmaus. The first two have the apostles as protagonists; in the last two models, Jesus is the agent of evangelization. These four models are to be taken as complementary in order to grasp the various dimensions of our mission of evangelization.[32]

Within the unity of a same objective, a same goal, there is room for various paths, indicated by the people we are addressing and by the person I am. There are different ways inspired by Jesus and the apostles to live one common mission. My presentations and reflections are driven by two questions that I would like a Christian reader to keep in mind in the course of reading this work. What does it mean for me to be a witness of God and of Jesus Christ in my milieu? How can the mission of Jesus and the apostles be a model for me in my own mission of bearing witness in the milieu where I live?

Chapter 2

Direct Proclamation of the Gospel
(The Kerygmatic Model)

The disciples of Jesus are called to pursue the mission that he entrusted to his apostles. In order to better grasp what is at the heart of this mission today—to appropriate its profound and lasting goal—we must "revisit" what is essential in the missionary witness of the apostles. This material is to be found in the missionary discourses of the Acts of the Apostles. The six discourses we find there are called kerygmas; translated literally from the Greek the term means "proclamation." The kerygma is the direct proclamation of Jesus Christ and the Gospel. We will look at the first of these discourses.

At the beginning of the Acts of the Apostles, the risen Jesus, after instructing the apostles he had chosen, tells them that they are going to receive a power, the power of the Holy Spirit, and adds that they will be his witnesses "not only in Jerusalem but throughout Judea and Samaria, and indeed to the ends of the earth" (Acts 1:8). The coming of the Holy Spirit is recounted at the beginning of chapter 2. It is the event of Pentecost. After this coming of the Spirit, Peter, in the name of the Twelve, gives the following testimony, which we read in Acts 2:

> 22"You who are Israelites, hear these words. Jesus the Nazorean was a man commended to you by God with mighty deeds, wonders, and signs, which God worked through him in your midst, as you yourselves know. 23This

man, delivered up by the set plan and foreknowledge of
God, you killed, using lawless men to crucify him. ²⁴But
God raised him up, releasing him from the throes of death,
because it was impossible for him to be held by it. ²⁵For
David says of him:

> 'I saw the Lord ever before me,
>> with him at my right hand I shall not be disturbed.
> ²⁶Therefore my heart has been glad and my tongue has
>> exulted;
>> my flesh, too, will dwell in hope,
> ²⁷because you will not abandon my soul to the nether-
>> world,
>> nor will you suffer your holy one to see corruption.
> ²⁸You have made known to me the paths of life;
>> you will fill me with joy in your presence.'

²⁹My brothers, one can confidently say to you about the
patriarch David that he died and was buried, and his tomb
is in our midst to this day. ³⁰But since he was a prophet and
knew that God had sworn an oath to him that he would
set one of his descendants upon his throne, ³¹he foresaw
and spoke of the resurrection of the Messiah, that neither
was he abandoned to the netherworld nor did his flesh
see corruption. ³²God raised this Jesus; of this we are all
witnesses. ³³Exalted at the right hand of God, he received
the promise of the holy Spirit from the Father and poured
it forth, as you [both] see and hear. ³⁴For David did not go
up into heaven, but he himself said:

> 'The Lord said to my Lord,
> "Sit at my right hand
>> ³⁵until I make your enemies your footstool."'

³⁶Therefore let the whole house of Israel know for certain
that God has made him both Lord and Messiah, this Jesus
whom you crucified."
    ³⁷Now when they heard this, they were cut to the heart,
and they asked Peter and the other apostles, "What are
we to do, my brothers?" ³⁸Peter [said] to them, "Repent

and be baptized, every one of you, in the name of Jesus Christ for the forgiveness of sins; and you will receive the Holy Spirit. [39]For the promise is made to you and to your children and to all those far off, whomever the Lord our God will call." [40]He testified with many other arguments, and was exhorting them, "Save yourselves from this corrupt generation." [41]Those who accepted his message were baptized, and about three thousand persons were added that day.

This discourse is thus the first of six evangelizing discourses addressed to a Jewish audience in the Acts of the Apostles. Chapters 2–13 offer six summaries of what can be called the first gospel preached in the church.[1] These "preaching plans" present the heart of the message of evangelization used by missionaries in the church during the time of the apostles as well as in the church today. These model discourses of primitive preaching are placed on the lips of Peter, except for the last one, which is attributed to Paul. They all resemble each other. We find, in one after the other, the same themes and the same outline.

Essentially, we could summarize the proclamation of the missionary disciples in the following way. During his life, Jesus of Nazareth was manifested as God's messenger by his words and by his deeds, which were of a unique character. However, he was not recognized as such. Rather, he was rejected and put to death. But God raised him up and we are witnesses to this. Therefore Jesus is the Christ, that is, the liberator announced in the Scriptures. Now there is hope for every human being: hope to be liberated from sin, that is, from the evil that assails us from outside and from within; hope to enter into a new life, which will not cease to grow in intensity and in quality; hope to belong to a new people called together by God. So, be converted, that is, change your way of seeing and your way of living; welcome Jesus, the Living One. Let yourselves be transformed by him and by his Spirit of life.

Peter concludes his discourse on Pentecost with this statement: "God has made this Jesus, whom you crucified, both Lord and Christ." This affirmation includes the two essential titles that proclaim who Jesus is at the deepest level.

- "Lord" (*kurios*): This is the title given to God in the Old Testament. The risen Jesus is Lord, that is, he is the One living from the life of God.

- "Christ": Messiah, the One who makes others live, who communicates the life of God.[2]

The person who believes in that, that is, who is converted—literally "turns toward" Jesus and welcomes him into his or her life—becomes a disciple of Jesus. He or she can then receive baptism, which is the sacrament of faith.[3]

The five other evangelizing discourses present substantially the same content. In each case particular aspects are developed in line with the kind of people who are addressed. For example, when speaking to Cornelius, a Roman centurion "who fears God," that is, who sympathizes with Judaism, who lives in Caesarea (Acts 10:1), and who probably did not know Jesus, Peter adds some details concerning the particular quality of Jesus' humanity: "Because God was with him, Jesus went about doing good and curing all who had fallen into the power of the devil" (Acts 10:38).

The kerygma proclaimed by the apostles presents the central message of the Christian faith. It is the Gospel, the "Good News" par excellence! In his pastoral letters, St. Paul reminds his Christian communities that it is this kerygma, centered on the risen Jesus, that he had announced to them and that remains the foundation of their faith. Note the following three passages:

> Now I am reminding you, brothers, of the gospel I preached to you, which you indeed received and in which you also stand. Through it you are also being saved, if you hold fast to the word I preached to you, unless you believed in vain.

> For I handed on to you as of first importance what I also received: that Christ died for our sins in accordance with the Scriptures; that he was buried; that he was raised on the third day in accordance with the Scriptures; that he appeared to Cephas, then to the Twelve. (1 Cor 15:1-5)

> For we do not preach ourselves, but Jesus Christ as Lord. (2 Cor 4:5)

> If you confess with your mouth that Jesus is Lord and believe in your heart that God raised him from the dead, you will be saved. (Rom 10:9)

The formula "Jesus is Lord (the One living forever) and Christ (the One who makes us live forever)" is the essential profession of the Christian faith.[4] Jesus is alive and he opens the way for us so that we might live eternally, beyond death, in a life of communion with him and with one another.

The witness must, at a given moment, proclaim the kerygma in the first person: "This is what 'I' believe." This is in fact what he or she does in prayers that end with the words, "Through Jesus Christ our Lord."

These discourses in the Acts of the Apostles testify to the evangelization the disciples of Jesus offered to Jews who were awaiting the coming of the Messiah. Thus, there are many references to the Holy Scriptures of the Jewish people, what we call the First (or Old) Testament. These references aim at showing that Jesus is indeed the longed-for Messiah of the people.

A Message of Hope

Evangelization has its place at the level of values, not ideas. Ideas do not mobilize people or motivate them to get involved or give their lives for a cause. Ideas do not convert.[5] Values mobilize. Of course, we have to transmit the Gospel by ideas and reflections. That is what we are doing in this volume. But we must be conscious that the ideas we transmit, the words we use to speak of the Gospel, will only have an impact on people if they connect with the values they want to live by or awaken in them values that they want to integrate into their lives.

What are the values that the apostles' kerygma touches or awakens in Jewish hearers? The one that seems most clear to me is, I believe, also the most profound: hope. This same value has the best chance of reaching people in our context today.

It is good to recall that, for the Jews, the coming of the Messiah meant the arrival of the kingdom of God, which had been announced by the prophets and thus channeled the hope of the people. The gospels show us that Jesus, by his words and by his deeds, made it clear that the kingdom of God had arrived in his person. By his entire life, he made visible that this kingdom was ultimately about love, which consisted in communion of human beings among themselves and with God. The arrival of this kingdom with the resurrection of Jesus is underlined in the Acts of the Apostles, as the following two texts, at the beginning and at the end of the book, indicate: "[he gave] instructions through the holy Spirit to the apostles whom he had chosen. He presented himself alive to them by many proofs after he had suffered, appearing to them during forty days and speaking about the kingdom of God" (Acts 1:2-3). Paul in Rome "with complete assurance and without hindrance . . . proclaimed the kingdom of God and taught about the Lord Jesus Christ" (Acts 28:31).[6]

Hope! In present circumstances our world has a hard time hoping. In his letter *At the Beginning of the New Millennium*, John Paul II, referring to new forms of poverty in the West, speaks of people "threatened by despair at the lack of meaning in their lives" (50).

The mission of the apostles, and that of the disciples of Jesus in their turn, is to testify that, since the time of Jesus and because of Jesus, there is hope. To each of us, to persons who lack hope, the resurrection of Jesus gives the most profound certitude:

• that evil will not have the last word in us or in the world.

- that this taste we have for living will not be frustrated, even if it seems more or less paralyzed today.

- that our deepest desires (the desire to know, to love, to live in truth, to become fully human) are not destined to come to nothing.

- that the frustrations, the failures, the sufferings that we live with now will not last; they will be ended with the fullness of the kingdom.

Above all, that is what the disciple of Jesus is: a person who, in a world that is often disenchanted and lacking in perspective, is a witness of hope. It is a woman or a man who gives a taste for living to those who are on the way to losing it. While the media are constantly announcing bad news, the disciple and witness of Jesus Christ, by his or her word, and even more so by his or her life, is a bearer of Good News. In a world that kills hope, disciples of Jesus say by their entire being: "Despite all that, there is hope." Jesus opens a future for us, a way of life, beyond our present frustrations. Because of the resurrection of Jesus, we know that life will win over death, love over hate, meaning over meaninglessness.

The event of Jesus is Good News *par excellence* for all human beings. Now there is hope for everyone: hope of being liberated from every form of evil—and first of all from the most radical human and spiritual evil: lack of love, which Scripture calls sin; hope of living a life of quality that will never finish growing, even beyond death: for if Jesus is risen, in him we are also called to the resurrection, as St. Paul tells us;[7] hope finally of living in love, in communion with others and with God, which is what the Gospel calls the life of the kingdom. The event of Jesus, therefore, gives profound meaning to human history and to each and every life on earth.

This witness to hope will only bear fruit, especially in secularized contexts, if we see Christians working to transform our present world in order to make it more human, more just, getting personally involved in a humanitarian cause in favor of the rights of marginalized people and in favor of peace. We will develop this point in the fourth chapter where we will examine a model of humanism in which Jesus, the model of compassion, is the great witness.

In his 2010 apostolic exhortation on the Word of God in the life and mission of the church, Benedict XVI wrote:

> What the Church proclaims to the world is the *Logos of Hope* (cf. 1 Pet 3:15); in order to be able to live fully each moment, men and women need "the great hope," which is the God who possesses a human face and who "has loved us to the end" (John 13:1). This is why the Church is missionary by her very nature. Everyone today, whether he or she knows it or not, needs this message. (*Verbum Domini* 91)

"Always be ready to give an explanation to anyone who asks you for a reason for your hope, but do it with gentleness and reverence" (1 Pet 3:15-16). This is the heart of the mission of evangelization!

Past, Present and Future

A great difficulty encountered today with regard to the faith in the secularized West, a difficulty that is not articulated but is present and very influential in people's attitudes, can be formulated in the following way: "Jesus Christ—and therefore the Church—all that is out of date! It has nothing to offer for us today or for our future!"

Traditional society—and the church!—has emphasized continuity, the time from past to present. Contemporary culture, on the other hand, is more interested in the time from the present to the future. For many people today, because the future is uncertain, all that matters is living in the present moment, in the provisional.

The faith of a disciple of Jesus is based on and rooted in an event that took place in the past: the event of the life, death, and resurrection of Jesus. But it is only the memory of a past event because this event is decisive for all human history. It is only interested in the past because it gives meaning to the present and looks to the future. Faith is concerned with Jesus Christ living in our world today.

It is hope in the future that makes us interested in the past, the event of Jesus. In a way, it is hope that leads to faith in Jesus Christ. Thus, the fundamental and decisive question concerning human presuppositions is not about belief in the past but hope in the future. Do we really want to share the future of Jesus, who is proclaimed as the firstfruits of our future? Opening ourselves to the Jesus event presupposes that we are, first of all, open to the hope of living and loving, which may be dormant but that dwells deep within each of us. In the end, we are beings of hope, as the poet Charles Péguy expressed it so well.[8] The kerygmatic proclamation should be an awakening of the taste for hope, of the desire to give meaning to life. With persons wounded by life, the taste for hope will first take the form of courage: to hope that in the end the future will be good and that on the earth itself it is possible to construct a more human world, despite all signs to the contrary in the past and in the present.

Relying on the forces of life such as love and freedom in us and around us is what opens up the meaning of the Jesus event and at the same time opens up meaning in light of that event. Then again, faith in this event lays the foundations for the hope that makes it work. It produces the certitude of a new future, a better future, which, although we are contributing to its construction according to our capacities, is received first of all from elsewhere, received gratefully as a gift.

Evangelization and Catechesis

The Acts of the Apostles show, however, that initial evangelization does not consist in doctrinal or moral instruction. Christian faith is not, first of all, adherence to a doctrinal content or moral values. Christian faith is essentially an encounter with Someone with whom one develops a relationship and by whom one lets oneself be transformed.[9] Of course, welcoming the person of Jesus Christ carries with it doctrinal and moral consequences. But these appear in a second moment, at the time of what we call catechesis. Just after the presentation of the kerygma made by Peter following the Pentecost event, the Acts of the Apostles goes on to present four essential values—we might call them four expressions of faithfulness—that nourished the first Christians after they came to believe in Jesus Christ and gave them the capacity to be a living and flourishing community: "They devoted themselves to the teaching of the apostles and to the communal life, to the breaking of the bread and to the prayers" (Acts 2:42). The first of these, "the teaching of the apostles," which in the Greek text is expressed by the term "didache," can be translated as "catechesis." The Acts recount of the apostles that "all day long, both at the temple and in their homes . . . they did not stop teaching and proclaiming the Messiah, Jesus" (Acts 5:42). The apostles worked on two fronts at the same time: before the non-Christians to whom they proclaimed the kerygma, the essential content of the Good News of Jesus Christ, and before the Christian community, whom they never stopped forming and instructing, giving them more profound teaching.

If there is no initial evangelization, if there is no personal relationship with God living in Jesus Christ, catechesis doesn't make any sense, since it represents delving deeper into the faith.[10] At this point I would like to add a more personal touch to my reflections. Today, where I come from (the largely secularized province of Quebec), who among those baptized in infancy and now under forty years of age have had the opportunity— the grace—to make a choice for Jesus Christ and to engage in personal prayer with him? I would say that the majority never received an initial evangelization. What will be the benefit of having a Catholic religious education at school if there is no foundation to integrate it into, that is, faith in the living Jesus?

Many young adults have received religious instruction—catechesis—that was part of their academic program in the public schools. But have they been evangelized? Have they been able to make a choice for faith in the risen Jesus? In other times this evangelization happened by a sort of osmosis in the family and in society. In their own way, parents and teachers gave witness to their faith. From childhood on, young people prayed in the family and at school. They made an act of faith in the living God, even if they had not received formal evangelization. Young adults today, when they become parents of young children, have lived through a social revolution that, for the majority of them, led to putting aside every form of religious practice.

For several years now, catechism is no longer included in the public school system of Quebec. It is now the responsibility of the parishes. Contacts with persons responsible for this catechesis and anecdotal reports from pastors give the impression that this catechesis takes place for the most part in an ambiance of faith. If the kerygma is not proclaimed directly, nonetheless it is a driving force in the presentations of the catechists. But how much longer will parents send their young children to catechesis if they themselves have not made a personal choice for Jesus Christ and consequently do not have any regular religious practice? And after receiving the sacraments of initiation, which may still motivate parents to send their children to catechism, how will the life of faith of these children be nourished if there is no family or parish practice to support the growth of the seeds of faith they are receiving in catechism?

Concentrating on What Is Essential in Evangelization

We have a lot of questions today about *how* to evangelize, *how* to bear witness, *how* to transmit the faith. These questions about *how* are very important, but the more fundamental question is *what—what* to transmit. We are no longer sure about *what* to transmit, and that is why we are so worried about the question of *how*. If we knew exactly *what* to communicate, it would be much easier to find the answer to *how*.

With regard to the question of what to communicate, we have to go to what is essential, what is most fundamental, what constitutes the heart of the Good News. This heart of the Gospel is given to us in the kerygma of the apostles, which must be interpreted and completed by the kerygma of Jesus. This we will examine later on (the evangelical model). The kingdom of God that Jesus preached is not primarily a collection of moral and social values. It is above all a Person. More exactly, the life of the kingdom of God includes an assortment of values for living that find their full meaning in their connection to the Person of the Living Jesus.[11]

In the West, many have left the church because religious practice, the sacraments, doctrine, and moral teaching of the church do not have meaning for them, since they do not rest on a living encounter with Jesus Christ.

A large number of those who are baptized have not been evangelized. People, and first of all the baptized, need to hear the kerygma at least one time in their life in a language that enables them to grasp its content and invites them to make a conscious personal choice. This proclamation of Jesus Christ should be proposed, not imposed. "How can they believe in him of whom they have not heard? And how can they hear without someone to preach?" (Rom 10:14).

The missionary witness of the apostles is very up to date for this mission. With a language adapted to our cultures and in relating it to our own situations, we need to recover the same dynamism that those first witnesses had and communicate the same substantial content of their founding testimony.

With the arrival of secularization, religion becomes a conscious choice rather than a heritage passively received. Thus secularization can be seen as an opportunity for us in the West, for it obliges us to go to the heart of the Gospel and of Christian faith, to the encounter with the risen Jesus.

I recall the survey conducted in France in 2007 in which only 18 percent of those who identify themselves as Catholics believe in a "personal God with whom they can enter into a relationship."[12] Most often the "Catholics" say they believe in a "Supreme Being" and in a life after death, without any mention of the risen Christ. That is deism, not Christian faith!

The kerygmatic proclamation should be at the heart of pastoral practice in the church—at the heart of preaching and of teaching given to the baptized people who come to our churches—and, from time to time, the members of the church should be invited to make a renewed personal choice for the living Jesus.[13]

This being said, if the kerygma of the apostles is the first reference for the goal of the mission, it is not necessarily the first reference for presenting the option of faith in a secularized world. Many people, especially in secularized contexts, are neither interested in nor ready for a direct proclamation of Jesus Christ. Certain individuals in the secularized world will be touched by such a proclamation, but the largest part of this world is either indifferent or strongly opposed.

In the Gospel of John, after the long discourse in which Jesus speaks of himself as "the bread of life eternal" (John 6:27-58), "many of his disciples returned to their former way of life and no longer accompanied him" (John 6:66). Jesus then asks his twelve apostles if they would go away too. Peter answers: "Master, to whom shall we go? You have the words of eternal life" (John 6:68). He puts in Jesus his hope for a life that continues after death. This response became in some way the response of the Christian West for centuries.[14] But today we can no longer say that the society and culture we live in believes in a life after death. Peter's response has to become personal for each of us. It is a choice that is no longer supported by communal culture and society.

Some Examples of Contemporary Kerygmatic Evangelization

When this direct proclamation of the kerygma is being done today, it is notably in certain public media. This phenomenon, which sociologists call a "Christianity of conversion," is growing in influence. There are about 200 million evangelical Christians and that figure is doubled if we include Pentecostals. This phenomenon is spreading especially among the masses in the Northern Hemisphere as well as in the Southern Hemisphere. In the West, it is spreading among immigrant populations. It reveals a spiritual hunger in many of our contemporaries. Studies have shown that what touches many at the deepest level, and especially among the poor in society, is the discovery of an immense personal love for them, manifested in Jesus Christ. This is for them a source of profound peace.

Some, even in our secularized societies, are thus drawn by the proclamation of a personal Savior. Personalizing the kerygma, inviting people to welcome Jesus as their Lord and personal Savior—that is what evangelical and Pentecostal preachers do. We can rejoice that people encounter Christ in these churches and are converted, but we have to deplore the fact that to experience this encounter and conversion, many have left the Catholic Church in which they were baptized.

We have to acknowledge that, thanks to its kerygmatic approach, the charismatic renewal has been in many places a grace for the Catholic Church; unfortunately, in some places, it has also manifested some limitations and in certain situations has strayed into questionable practices. In the Catholic Church, the international movement *Evangelization 2000* uses the media to offer a direct proclamation of the kerygma. This crusade undoubtedly has some good elements and some not-so-good elements. Its success depends on the contexts in which it is used.

Nonetheless, we should note a limitation of this kerygmatic proclamation. Many fundamentalist evangelical preachers give no consideration to the humanizing and social dimensions of the faith. They present Christ the Savior, but they forget the

Jesus of the gospels. Everything is centered on the message: "Jesus is your Savior. Acknowledge that you are a sinner." Their use of the Bible is fundamentalist and its interpretation often subjective.[15]

On the other hand, several years ago I was fascinated by reading a story about a Catholic missionary, Fr. Vincent Donovan, who made use of the kerygmatic approach in presenting the faith to the Masai people of Tanzania in East Africa. These people had benefited for a very long time from the educational and social services offered by the Catholic mission there, but no one had ever become a Christian. Fr. Donovan went to villages where "traditional" religion was practiced, and with the approval of the chief, gathered the people of the village on a regular basis to present Jesus Christ to them. He then helped the community to reflect on and discuss what to do about the message. Many of the villagers opted for Jesus Christ and became Christians.[16] Other places, other customs . . . no doubt!

Symbolic Language

It seems to me that an in-depth study of the evangelizing discourses of the first thirteen chapters of the Acts of the Apostles leads to the following conclusion: the language of evangelization in a Jewish milieu is a language of midrash. I believe I demonstrated this clearly with regard to Paul's discourse in the synagogue of Antioch in Pisidia.[17] My study led me to identify enough parallel elements in the other discourses to the Jews to conclude that this is the case for all evangelical preaching in the cultural world of Judaism. Now the language of midrash is a form of symbolic language.

The language of midrash was widely used in the culture of ancient Judaism. Midrash is essentially a discourse intended to reinterpret a passage of Scripture in light of a new event, to uncover a hidden sense, previously unknown, of a Scripture text in a new socio-historical situation. It is in the meeting of two lights, the light of a Scripture from the past and the light of a current event, that the meaning emerges.

Take an example: the missionary discourse of Paul in the synagogue of Antioch in Pisidia (Acts 13:16-41). On a first reading of the text, and even more so after a careful study of the structure of the discourse, a rather surprising discovery materializes: in this discourse, which is a kerygmatic proclamation of Jesus Christ, a large part of the text is given over to citations of and allusions to the Old Testament.[18] A key term in Paul's address is the past "promise" made to King David concerning a successor who would secure his sovereignty.[19] Paul's entire address appears to be an exposition and an actualized fulfillment of the Old Testament Scripture, more precisely the prophetic passage found in 2 Samuel 7:6-16. The language of the Christian orator is essentially that of Judaism. Paul borrows a form of speech and a content of thought that are those of his Jewish audience. He recounts the Jesus event in terms of their culture, of their existing religious understanding, of the longing and hope central to their faith, that is, the accomplishment of liberation and the coming of a new David.

In analyzing more closely the midrashic argumentation of St. Paul, it is clear that he draws out from Scripture passages, from the cultural and religious values of the people, from the hope of those who hear him, a new depth of meaning. A recent event—the resurrection of Jesus—serves as catalyst: it makes a new meaning spring up from an old one. Procedurally, the whole argument is constructed on amphibology (an ambiguous grammatical structure that conveys a double meaning) manifested by the terms used in the argument: thus the promise to "raise up" a new David has become a reality in the "raising up"—the resurrection—of Jesus.[20]

If we continue our reflection on the results of this exegesis, one conclusion seems evident: the language of evangelization for a Jewish audience is a symbolic language. We understand the concept of symbol in the sense of definitions by several contemporary philosophers, such as Jean Ladrière and Paul Ricoeur: the symbol is characterized by the semantic structure of a double meaning; a second meaning is intended by means of and through a first meaning.[21] And so it is with the discourse of evangelization: it is essentially a use of double meaning; by use of terms with multiple meanings (for example, the vocabulary of "raising up" (*anistēmi, egeirō* in Acts 13), realities that constitute a society (in the case of the Jews, the Scripture, the promise, their history) are called upon to render a new depth of meaning. In their first meaning, they evoke, and in a mysterious way, they "aim at" Christian reality.

In the missionary discourses delivered to the Jews in the Acts of the Apostles, the Christian meaning is in the end the product of fusing the Jewish cultural horizon and the Jesus event.[22] It is not the case today where cultures are no longer religious, or more precisely, are not waiting for a messiah.[23] But the symbolic dimension can still work, though in a different manner. Christian faith needs to be inscribed in the human quest of all periods and of all cultures. The apostles themselves were called to live this inculturation when they passed from the Jewish world to other worlds of the vast Roman empire of their day. The discourses of Paul at Lystra and at Athens in the Acts of the Apostles are a valuable indicator for us.

Conclusion

What we should recall concerning the direct approach to the proclamation of the kerygma is that at a moment when evangelization is set in motion, the Christian witness needs to talk about Jesus Christ and the Gospel. People have the right to hear the Word of the Gospel. It is not enough to bear witness only by the way we live.[24] The Word of the Gospel goes beyond our human words and has its own efficaciousness, its own fruitfulness!

On the other hand, the testimony of the Word and the testimony of life are complementary. In the Acts of the Apostles, the proclamation of the Word took full effect with people because it was accompanied by a testimony of life. The quality of life of the first communities had a great power of attraction and witnessing. On this subject we need to reread the summary statements in the Acts of the Apostles.[25]

The kerygmatic discourses present the missionary goal, but not a missionary pedagogy that would generally be appropriate for the world today, particularly in secularized countries. People today are allergic to those who pretend to possess the truth and proclaim it to them. Secularized people, in general, are not ready to hear us speak about Jesus as Christ, Lord, Savior, and Son of God. We need another approach if we want to reach them, to touch their minds and especially their hearts: an approach in stages, starting where they are, with their quest, with their capacity to receive. We need to wait for and seize the *kairos*, the opportune moment, to proclaim the Risen Jesus, Christ and Lord.

We will speak about evangelization in stages. And for that, I see not only one model in the New Testament but several.

Chapter 3

The Athens Model

B efore examining a new model for evangelization in the early days of the church, it will be good to recall a few elements of the content and structure of the book of the Acts of the Apostles.

This book is constructed around the figures of two apostles, Peter and Paul. The first part, the first twelve chapters, could be called "The Acts of Peter," and the second part, chapters 13-28, could be called "the Acts of Paul." The first part unfolds entirely in the Jewish world and gives us five kerygmatic discourses of Peter (in chapters 2-10), all addressed to a Jewish audience. After chapter 12 Peter reappears only for a brief intervention at the Council of Jerusalem, where he supports Paul and Barnabas in their proposal not to impose circumcision and the law on new converts coming from paganism (Acts 15:7-11). The first part of Acts recounts the conversion of St. Paul, as well as the revelation of his vocation to bear witness to the Lord not only among Jews but also to the pagan nations (Acts 9:1-19).

The second part shows Paul sent on mission by the church established at Antioch in Syria (Acts 13:1-4). Paul first addresses the Jews living in the diaspora. His preaching is of the same style as the kerygma proclaimed by Peter, as we can see from his missionary discourse in the synagogue of Antioch in Pisidia (Acts 13:16-41). But, confronted by the quite general rejection of their message by the Jews, Paul and his companion Barnabas understand that they are called to bring the Gospel to all the nations (Acts 13:46). Nonetheless, they never stop bearing witness to Jesus Christ before the Jews when the occasion arises (Acts 28:17-24).

An Approach Rooted in Greek Culture

When Paul leaves the Jewish world to begin the mission in the world of Greek culture, he makes a radical change in his missionary approach, as we can see in the two model discourses that Luke presents to us: the one in Lystra (Acts 14:15-17) and especially the one in Athens (Acts 17:22-31). In addressing Jews, the apostles started with the Jewish hope, their desire for the Messiah, and announced Jesus as the Messiah they were waiting for. The Greeks were not waiting for the Messiah—and in that respect *we* are Greeks—but they were looking for something else. In Athens Paul starts with their quest: "an unknown God." He gives his address in the public square—where the people are. In speaking about God, he uses the language of popular philosophy, Stoicism, and he cites the Greek poets. His evangelization is truly inserted in the ambient culture. It is inculturated.

Before meditating on the text of the discourse at Athens, we will look briefly first at an evangelizing discourse that Paul delivered in a "pagan"—i.e., non-Jewish—milieu. By the term "pagan," we mean a milieu whose population was not Jewish but was religious—more precisely, they believed in divinities—as did all people of that time. This brief missionary discourse, pronounced at Lystra, a city influenced by Hellenist civilization, serves the literary function in the Acts of the Apostles of preparing for the longer discourse that Paul will address to the Athenians in chapter 17.

The Discourse at Lystra (Acts 14:15-17)

In the course of their first missionary journey, Paul and Barnabas arrive at a small rural city called Lystra. As they had done in other cities, they also announced the Good News there. Now an event occurred during their stay in Lystra: Paul saw that one of his hearers, who had been crippled from birth, had the faith to be saved. He cured him. When they saw this miracle, the people decided that Paul and Barnabas were gods come down from heaven ("They called Barnabas 'Zeus' and Paul 'Hermes,' because he was the chief speaker," v. 12). The priest of Zeus, with the approval of the crowd, wanted to offer a sacrifice. This is the context in which Paul and Barnabas give the following missionary testimony, which is recounted for us in the Acts of the Apostles at chapter 14 (verses 15-17):

> [15]Men, why are you doing this? We are of the same nature as you, human beings. We proclaim to you Good News that you should turn from these idols to the living God, 'who made heaven and earth and sea and all that is in them.' [16]In past generations he allowed all Gentiles to go their own ways; [17]yet, in bestowing his goodness, he did not leave himself without witness, for he gave you rains from heaven and fruitful seasons, and filled you with nourishment and gladness for your hearts.

The discourse at Lystra is very brief and quite sober, but rich in meaning. After saying that they are human beings exactly like the people they are addressing, the missionaries start their exposition. They have come to announce "Good News." This "Gospel" contains two messages: on the one hand, an exhortation to abandon this foolishness (literally, "these vain things"), that is, belief in idols and sacrifices offered to creatures, and on the other hand, a call to turn to the living God. Receiving the second message implies abandoning belief in idols and sacrifices to creatures. Let us consider the second message that covers most of this little discourse.

The Living God toward whom Paul invites the nations to turn—nations represented here by the population of Lystra—is characterized by three affirmations: he is the Creator God

(v. 15c), he allowed the nations to follow their own ways (v. 16), and he has unceasingly given indications of his existence by granting various benefits to people (v. 17). These three qualifications of God are expressed by this Judeo-Christian in terms borrowed from the Old Testament, but the reality they evoke was also known in the Hellenistic world. What is new here is the expansion of the second and third qualities. While in the perspective of Judaism the providence and benevolence of God (v. 16-17) was seen as reserved to the Jewish people, the chosen people, Paul sees them as granted to all the nations. The true God, the living God, creator of all that exists, enters into relations with all human beings and is interested in the life of all the nations, allowing all of them to go their own way. Thus, every human being can enter into a relationship with God who is already present to him or her.

Note in particular, at verse 16, the meaning of the verb "follow" and of the noun "ways" is positive or neutral, but not negative: in the past, God allowed all nations to follow their own ways of living, their own ways of life. These ways were not without religious experience, even if they may have been strewn with errors like idolatry (v. 15b). The living God has, in some way, allowed people to follow the ways that they had chosen for living and growing, even with the risk of straying. God always accompanied people in their history.

The Good News announced by Paul and Barnabas is thus a call to abandon sacrifices to created idols and to receive the living God, whose existence is seen in all of creation, in the history of their communities, and in the daily life of their people.[1] The apostles invite them to a monotheistic faith. They affirm that the living God does not give signs of his presence only to the Jews, but that he has his ways of manifesting his presence and his benevolence to the Gentiles as well, that is, to all the peoples of the earth. Their message is indeed "Good News."

Note also that the Good News announced to the "Gentiles" of Lystra is only about conversion to the living God and there is at this point no message about faith in the risen Jesus. This testimony is theocentric, not Christocentric. It is "Good News," but it is not complete.

The Discourse at Athens (Acts 17:22-31)

After traversing Asia Minor, Paul and his missionary companion cross over to Europe. They visit various places in what was then called Macedonia and what today is Greece. They arrive at Athens, the capital of Greek culture. There Paul delivers the following discourse, which we find in chapter 17 of the Acts of the Apostles.

> [22]Then Paul stood up at the Areopagus and said: "You Athenians, I see that in every respect you are very religious. [23]For as I walked around looking carefully at your shrines, I even discovered an altar inscribed, 'To an Unknown God.' What therefore you unknowingly worship, I proclaim to you. [24]The God who made the world and all that is in it, the Lord of heaven and earth, does not dwell in sanctuaries made by human hands, [25]nor is he served by human hands because he needs anything. Rather it is he who gives to everyone life and breath and everything.
>
> [26]He made from one the whole human race to dwell on the entire surface of the earth, and he fixed the ordered seasons and the boundaries of their regions, [27]so that people might seek God, even perhaps grope for him and find him, though indeed he is not far from any one of us.
>
> [28]For 'In him we live and move and have our being,' as even some of your poets have said, 'for we too are his offspring.' [29]Since therefore we are the offspring of God, we ought not to think that the divinity is like an image fashioned from gold, silver, or stone by human art and imagination. [30]God has overlooked the times of ignorance, but now he demands that all people everywhere repent [31]because he has established a day on which he will 'judge the world with justice' through a man he has appointed,

and he has provided confirmation for all by raising him from the dead." [32]When they heard about resurrection of the dead, some began to scoff, but others said, "We should like to hear you on this some other time." [33]And so Paul left them. [34]But some did join him, and became believers. Among them were Dionysius, a member of the Court of the Areopagus, a woman named Damaris, and others with them.

Is This Really a Model of Evangelization?

Before commenting on this discourse, we should clarify a point concerning our perception of it. An interpretation long transmitted in Christian churches, especially Protestant churches, but also in Catholic churches, runs as follows: Paul's discourse at Athens was a failure and as a result Paul decided not to use human wisdom (for example, the popular philosophy of Stoicism that he had used at Athens), but to preach "the folly of the cross" (1Cor 1:18ff.). In support of this interpretation, they cite the passage in Paul's first letter to the Corinthians: "When I came to you, brothers, proclaiming the mystery of God, I did not come with sublimity of words or of wisdom. For I resolved to know nothing while I was with you except Jesus Christ, and him crucified" (1 Cor 2:1-2).[2]

This interpretation was widely spread in French-speaking milieus by a number of exegetes, following the publication in 1935 by a respected author, A.-J. Festugière.[3] It still appears in the writings of exegetes. Two editions of the Bible that are widely used in French-speaking contexts, *The Jerusalem Bible* (editions of 1973 and 1998), allude to it and seem to endorse it. Today the tendency of writings and commentaries coming from exegetes is to reject this line of interpretation and to recognize that Luke, in the Acts of the Apostles, presents in Acts 17 a model of evangelizing discourse in the pagan Greek environment.[4]

In our opinion, Luke, in the Acts of the Apostles, presents the missionary discourse of Paul at Athens as a model of evangelization, like the other missionary discourses of Peter and Paul that he recounts in the preceding chapters of his book. In support of this affirmation, we will look at the following points:

- First of all, the argument presented to assert that the discourse at Athens should not be considered a model is fallacious. In fact, it is not a good method to interpret a text redacted by Luke by another text coming from the hand of Paul (the letter to the Corinthians). The context, the objective, and the meaning of the terms used do not have the same bearing in the two passages.

- In the Acts of the Apostles, Luke wants to show the progress of the Gospel from a Jewish context to the pagan world, including all humanity (Acts 1:8). To achieve this project he gives typical examples of missionary preaching.

- Look at the end of the discourse at Athens: "When they heard about resurrection of the dead, some began to scoff" (Acts 17:32). Some members of the audience laugh at the mention of the resurrection of the dead, but not at the main points of the discourse.

- The reaction of the audience at the end of the discourse is not a clear and unanimous rejection of Paul's message. Rather, the hearers are divided, as elsewhere in the Acts of the Apostles, upon hearing the missionary preaching. In Greek the sentence is clear enough on this subject: *"hoi men . . . hoi de,"* that is, "on the one hand," some laughed, "on the other hand," some expressed the desire to hear more from Paul on this subject (v. 32).[5]

- Following the text of the discourse at the Areopagus, Luke says explicitly that "some became believers," among them are counted two persons who are undoubtedly important, since Luke bothers to identify them by name: Dionysius the Areopagite and a woman named Damaris "and others with them" (v. 34).

- At Athens, the reaction to Paul's preaching is as good as, if not better than, what he had received at the end of his missionary preaching in the synagogue of Antioch in Pisidia, which Luke presents in the Acts of the Apostles as a model of evangelization in a Jewish context (Acts 13:14-41). There it is said that upon leaving the synagogue, "they invited them to speak on these subjects the following Sabbath" and that "many Jews and worshipers who were converts to Judaism followed Paul and Barnabas" and that "Paul and Barnabas . . . urged them to remain faithful to the grace of God" (Acts 13:42-44; cf. 13:52). "The Jews, however, incited the women of prominence who were worshipers and the leading men of the city, stirred up a persecution against Paul and Barnabas, and expelled them from their territory" (Acts 13:50). According to the author of the Acts of the Apostles, it is normal that the missionary preaching, which had to be inculturated, effectively touched some hearers and left others indifferent. In certain situations, the missionary witness can provoke hostility, as was the case at Antioch in Pisidia.

Explanation of the Discourse at Athens

Athens was the university city par excellence and there Paul addressed an audience that was highly cultivated and profoundly marked by the Stoic philosophy popular at the time. For Luke this missionary discourse represents the encounter of the Gospel with Greek culture.

As at Lystra, the theme of the speech is not centered on the presentation of the risen Jesus, Christ and Lord, but aims at raising consciousness of God in nature and in daily life. Unlike Lystra, the discourse at Athens refers to Jesus at the very end, but it does not present him as the Messiah, unlike the evangelizing discourse directed to a Jewish audience. Rather, it appears as a way to help us understand something of the very being of this God whom we aspire to know.[6]

To sum up, we need to raise the following points in Paul's approach: he begins by recognizing what is positive in the religious culture of the Athenians, steeped in Stoicism. They are "very religious," they know God "who made the world and all that is in it," "the Lord of heaven and earth." Paul enters into their spiritual quest, which their altar to the "Unknown God" manifests. And so he starts with their desire to know about the God who is "unknown" to them. He announces that God is not far off from each of them. In the end he introduces Jesus who reveals fully who is the real God whom they desire to know at the deepest level. Some reject this proposal, some want to know more, others become believers (Acts 17:32-34).

We will look at the orator's method in a more detailed manner but must begin with an observation. In order to grasp the richness of the argumentation in the missionary discourse at Athens, we must remember that Paul was a product of two cultures: the Jewish culture, nourished by the First (or Old) Testament, and Greek culture through his education at Tarsus. The missionary discourse at Athens reveals that the author has a good knowledge not only of the Hebrew Scriptures; he was also well acquainted with the poets and the Stoic philosophers whose thought permeated the popular culture of the Athenians.[7] Paul makes use of concepts and employs terminology that, while having a biblical resonance, was nonetheless familiar to his Athenian audience. This is a good example of "transcultural" evangelization: what makes sense for the orator in his (Jewish) cultural horizon now has to make sense for his hearers in their own sociocultural (Greek) horizon at Athens.

Some Themes Current in the Stoicism of that Period

If we put ourselves in the place of his Greek hearers, the speech makes good sense. In fact, it is with Greek thought that connections are spontaneously made. At the beginning of his discourse, Paul speaks of the "cosmos" (v. 24), a term that was current in Hellenism and appears several times in the Greek version of the Old Testament.[8] The statement that God "does not dwell in sanctuaries made by human hands" (v. 24), that he is not "served by human hands" and "does not need anything" (v. 25) brings to mind passages from Xenophon and Euripides, and especially themes dear to the stoic philosophers like Zeno, Seneca, and Epictetus.[9] The stoics proclaimed that God "gives to everyone life and breath and everything" (v. 25), that he is not someone distant (v. 27) and that it is everyone's vocation to look for him (v. 27).[10] The heart of Paul's argument is verse 28, constructed from references to two Greek poets: "In him we live and move and have our being" is likely a reference to the poet Epimenides of Crete, and "we too are his offspring" is a citation taken from the stoic poet Aratos.[11] Even the Greek verb *metanoein* at the end of the discourse (v. 30) seems to have more the Greek sense of "changing one's way of seeing" than the typical biblical sense of "repenting" (especially when we consider the statement at the beginning of verse 30: "God has overlooked the time of ignorance"). The theological points of emphasis on God the Creator (v. 24), the benevolent director (v. 26), and just judge (v. 31) are in line with the popular Hellenistic theodicy proposed by Stoicism.

Thus, almost all the major points of Paul's missionary address evoke themes current in Stoicism, the philosophy that had become popular at the time. Its vocabulary and thought had permeated all levels of society, in a way similar to the way Marxism did in certain countries in the course of the twentieth century.[12] The whole missionary discourse, therefore, could have been understood by a Greek who had no knowledge of the Old Testament.

Another Horizon of Meaning

On the other hand, the drift of the discourse is also well anchored in the horizon of meaning of the Judeo-Christian missionary. One can take each of the verses and find parallels in the considerable literature of the Old Testament. The discourse will then appear as an exposition to the nations of biblical monotheism—of the one, provident God of the Old Testament—and as a critique of idolatry, following a model of thought familiar in the Old Testament (Wis 13–15). The affirmation that God is close to human beings, because "we too are his offspring" (vv. 27-28), recalls the biblical theme of human beings created in the image of God as much as it does the Stoic idea of the soul as related to God. In verse 26, the Greek expression, here translated as "he fixed the ordered seasons and the boundaries of their regions," is ambiguous: the reference can refer either to the historical providence of God with regard to the lives of nations, as we find in the Old Testament, or the order of the seasons as a manifestation of God, in line with Stoicism. In the original Greek text, the beginning of the same verse 26 says simply, "He made from one the whole human race," without further specification, which can mean either "from one single principle" (Stoicism) or "from one single man" (Gen 1). The human vocation to look for God can be understood as a search of the mind (which makes sense in Hellenism) and as a quest of the heart and will (in line with the Old Testament). Two horizons of meaning make up the dynamic of this dialogue of evangelization. The missionary discourse, which is the expression of a true intercultural encounter, is thus by its very nature polysemic (having multiple meanings).[13]

Continuity and Discontinuity

Another point to mention about this model missionary discourse at Athens: as well as for evangelization in the Jewish milieu (the missionary discourses from Acts 2 to Acts 13), there is continuity between the religious culture of the hearers and the Gospel, but there is also, and even more so in a non-Jewish context, discontinuity and innovation. The Good News contains a critique of certain religious practices of the world of the nations, notably idolatry. The orator makes clear to his audience a contradiction between their deep desire for a creator God within and their devotion to manmade gods outside. He strives to make them understand that they have to abandon their empty idols (Acts 17:29; 17:16) and fix their regard on the only true God. He shows that these two ways of seeing God are incompatible: if they choose the first, which belongs to the best of their culture (he is referring to their poets and alluding to their thinkers), they must reject the second: "Since therefore we are offspring of God, we ought not to think . . ." (v. 29). The principal point of Paul's argument is, unambiguously, the personal God (*ho theos*, v. 30). But curiously, it is not Paul who proclaims it: it is God who "now . . . demands that all people everywhere repent" (v. 30). The decisive revelation, or rather the invitation to take the decisive step of conversion, is it reserved to God himself?

A Theocentric Discourse

At the very end of this entirely theocentric discourse, in the last verse, Paul turns the attention—we might simply say the curiosity—of his hearers to the person of Jesus. The presentation of the man Jesus as risen and as the instrument of the judgment made by God does not seem to rest on any foundation of what Hellenism is expecting. The discourse at Athens attests that the Good News concerning Jesus Christ makes no sense if it does not rest on a faith in and a cult dedicated to the true God, which excludes every idolatrous practice.[14]

Finally, we may note that the principal teaching of this discourse is not about salvation, but about knowledge of the true God, presented as the creator of all and Lord (Acts 17:24). Paul emphasizes the nearness of the presence of God to human beings, expressed in terms familiar to the philosophical and religious thought of Stoicism: he "gives to everyone life and breath and everything" (v. 25); "in him we live, and move, and have our being;" "we too are his offspring" (v. 28). The last verse of the speech alludes to an intervention of God who "will judge the world with justice." On what is this judgment based? Does it rest on the knowledge of the true God, as the development of the discourse would seem to indicate? Or, from a larger perspective, does it rest on human action, as is generally the case in Biblical language about judgment? We cannot answer this question.

We can draw from this discourse the following reflection. In his missionary testimony, Paul uses the cultural language of the people and he starts with their experience, with their personal quest. He recognizes that the Greeks of Athens are very religious (v. 22), that they already have a certain experience of the true God—for they worship him without knowing it—although their knowledge of this true God may be deficient and may contain aberrations. They can nonetheless acquire a sound knowledge of the true God if, leaving aside the idols, they deepen their search for him who, as a parent, is present to them at the deepest level of their being. This is what the poets and philosophers of their religious culture are indicating. The complete transformation of their present state of ignorance—transformation that will have consequences for their religious practice—will take place to the extent that they receive the Word that God is proclaiming to them now (vv. 30-31). That will happen, as verses 30-31 imply, if they open their hearts and minds to the knowledge of the risen Jesus who will fully reveal to them who the real God is.[15]

An Inculturated Faith

The analysis of Paul's missionary discourses at Lystra and Athens, following upon the analysis of Peter's discourse at Jerusalem, brings to light the fact that the disciples began, in their witnessing, with the experience of the people they were addressing: their culture, their expectations and hopes, but also the gaps and the narrow vision in which they were enclosed.

The comparison of the missionary discourses delivered to Jews (Acts 2–13) with those proclaimed to pagans (Acts 14 and 17) allows us to grasp more clearly that evangelization needs to be adapted to each person and his or her culture.

At Lystra and at Athens, Paul experimented with a way of evangelizing that we might call transcultural. He, who had experienced an encounter with Jesus Christ in the language and the religious culture of Judaism in which he was raised, was called to bear witness in a language and a religious culture of people formed in an entirely different world. Is it not true that a similar experience of "transculturation" is needed in our context today, in a secularized world? Have we not passed from a culture permeated with religious terms and references to a culture in which these terms and references no longer have a place, and if we use them, do they not ring true for a vast majority of those who hear them?

Undoubtedly, the Greeks of Athens who became Christians were gradually transformed by their reception of the Gospel. But they also stamped this Gospel with the seal of who they were. They certainly thought and lived the Gospel, the same faith in Jesus Christ and in the God it reveals, in a different way from the first Christians who came from the Jewish people.

In this discourse of evangelization for Greek hearers, the author of the Acts of the Apostles presents a model of what we would call today "the inculturation" of the faith.[16] Inculturation is part of the very nature of the Christian faith as a universal religion. One same faith is called to be lived in all cultures and therefore to take on a variety of socio-cultural and religious expressions according to time and place. The Christian faith is always expressed within a culture, but it is inseparably linked to none, not even to the one in which it was born, Jewish culture. It can therefore be embodied in all cultures.[17] As the common reference accepted by all believers, the Gospel will be reflected upon and lived out in a different manner in various times and cultures.

The discourses at Lystra and Athens show us clearly the direction to take in our missionary work: because the Gospel is destined to the entire world, it can in no way be expressed in terms of a single culture (European, Asian, or African, for example) or in the categories of a single social class or a single gender.

The Spirit "blows where it wills" (John 3:8). In his own way, Paul, at Athens, recognized what was positive in the religious culture of the Athenians (Stoicism). Obviously, we would only recognize in this opening a rough sketch of a process that today would be called interreligious dialogue.[18]

A reader who wants to study this discourse in greater depth can proceed to the more detailed analysis of this text that I published in the review *Eglise et Théologie*.[19]

Starting with Contemporary Spiritual Quests

What about us? How do we speak about our faith and bear witness to it today? Paul departed from the Jewish language and culture, and putting himself, so to speak, in the shoes of his hearers, used their words and their way of thinking, their culture, and their quest to testify to his faith. This is a good invitation to us Christians today, to get beyond our own religious terminology, the answers we learned in catechism, and to try to find new ways of thinking, new ways of speaking, of posing questions, and of understanding the anxieties and the personal quests of those around us. However, this cannot become an excuse for not seeking to know and understand the content of our faith. On the contrary, the more we deepen our faith, the more we become free with regard to the formulas we learned in order to express the essential contents in concepts and words that can reach people in our cultures today.[20]

Nonetheless, not every cultural and linguistic reality can open the door onto Christian reality. The God who is proclaimed should be perceived as beyond and in opposition to all the idols that human beings are inclined to fashion. And he should be understood at one and the same time as transcendent (creator) and immanent (intimately present to everyone).

The document of the assembly of the bishops of Quebec, published in 1999, *Annoncer l'Évangile dans la culture actuelle au Québec* (Proclaiming the Gospel in the Present Culture in Quebec), describes in a poignant way the cultural transformations that have marked Quebec's society in the course of recent years. It notes that the weak impact the proclamation of the Gospel has today is due to "the widening gap between ecclesial practices and contemporary culture" (Introduction).

Today many people in the West are sensitive to a language that starts with the divine dimension of the human person or a language that speaks of a cosmic God, the kind of language Paul used at Athens. This type of approach will have an effect with a good number of people in the secularized world today who are drawn to "New Age" thought or those who are in search of a "spiritual dimension,"[21] "God who is closer to me than I am to myself," as St. Augustine puts it.[22]

Generally speaking, for those living in the West, the term "spirituality" is much more in favor than the term "religion." The latter term is undoubtedly too much associated with practices of piety, duties to perform, and moral prohibitions. The term "spirituality" is more nebulous, with more fluid content. However, for many people who say that they do not belong to any religion, the spiritual quest remains present within them as a quest for the divine. One who bears witness to the God of Jesus Christ should be attentive to this type of quest, to this divine that, for some, is identified with the "Self" described by the psychoanalyst Carl Jung.[23] This can be a starting point.

Apart from institutional religion, new movements of human and spiritual growth are attractive to many because they speak about the beauty and the grandeur of the human person. They disclose a person's latent potential. These movements can then be seen by the Christian evangelizer as partners rather than competitors or adversaries. In their own way, they can be partners in raising consciousness about the unimagined value of the human being, created in the image of God. They offer an invitation to speak first of all in positive terms about human persons, to highlight their qualities rather than concentrate on their weaknesses. Doing this, the first language of the disciples of Jesus will be more like the discourse of their Master: in words, a proclamation of the Gospel as "Good News," and in attitudes and actions, a positive appreciation of every person, starting with what is best in him or her.

The Way of Interiority

Christianity, in its long tradition, has recognized a variety of ways to God. The way of otherness, the encounter with God by encountering the other, is highly esteemed at the present time, and rightly so. We will speak about this in the next chapter. Nonetheless, should we not also recognize the value of another way, also traditional, that many people who are engaged in a spiritual quest outside the church find helpful today: the way of interiority? The Christian acknowledges that the liberating God is first of all a creator God: he is the one who gives to all living things "life, movement and being" and "who is not far from each of us," as Paul tells the Athenians, who were largely influenced by a pantheistic view of the world.[24] The Christian disciple should avoid an image widely used in talk about evangelization, where evangelizing is seen as bringing God to the world. God is already there. We want to reveal him, or more precisely, we want to help people recognize his presence.

The way of interiority is much in use today. A survey published in France in 2007 (cited in the first chapter) reported that 25 percent of those who belong to the Catholic Church say they pray at least once a week; this is three times the number of those who say they attend Sunday Mass every week.[25] Many people, often without any attachment to a religious tradition, have a thirst for silence and interiority; they have a developed spiritual life and, with regard to the Christian tradition, they could even be said to be mystics, a term much too long reserved to a very small minority. Some of these people have had very profound experiences through practices of Oriental schools of spirituality and they desire to reconnect with the Christianity in which they were baptized. This return to their first tradition will only be possible if they feel that their religious experiences outside of that tradition are understood and respected.

The thirst for the spiritual has its source in the fact that every human being is created in the image of God and is thus deeply engaged in a quest for God. The Christian knows this by revelation (see Gen 1:26). As a witness he or she is called to awaken this profound quest in others and to nurture it.[26]

But, like Paul, the witnessing disciple helps people discover that the response to their quest for the divine is not found only within themselves. It is found in welcoming God who is Other, the personal God with whom we enter into relationship, who alone can really satisfy our desire to live and to love.

The fruitful dialogue between a witness of Jesus Christ and a person engaged in a quest for a spiritual life presupposes openness on the part of both of them. At Athens, Paul's hearers acknowledged the unknown god in their pantheon and they were disposed to hear a message coming from elsewhere (Acts 17:19-23).

At first, the quest for spirituality often takes the form of a search for meaning: the meaning of life, the meaning of death. Many of those today who do not belong to any religious confession pose these questions at one or another moment in their lives: "What am I living for? Why do I die?" This can lead to the birth of another question: "And if God existed?" This question of God as the foundation of all things—the unknown God—can arise when they recognize the emptiness of the idols they have created.

Challenges for the Church and for Christians

In the eyes of many of our contemporaries, the church does not appear to be a place for a spiritual life. The principal image that Catholicism reflects in society—and even for many Catholics—is of an institution that is the guardian of moral codes. Beyond the institution and morality (these need to be presented in their own proper place, but that place is not the stage where evangelization is done), the disciples of Jesus Christ are invited to help surface both in the social conscience and especially in the life of Christians themselves the fundamental objective of a commitment to the Christian faith: to have a genuine spiritual experience, the experience of an encounter with God as well as the inner transformation that goes with it. Cut off from their spiritual dimension, the institutional and moral dimensions of Christianity lose their firm foundation and their ultimate goal. It is not surprising that their social impact is also diminished.

New spiritual trends oblige Christians to define what is specific to them and to focus on what is essential. You have to know who you are and what is essential in your belief in order to dialogue with someone who is different without losing your own identity.

The witnessing disciple is called to develop what Paul sketches out at the end of his discourse at Athens: the God in whom he believes and to whom he bears witness is a personal God, who is Love and who has only one desire, which is to enter into communion with the humans he created. Thus it is only in responding to the love of God that we truly come to know God, to encounter God. To know how a human responds to the love of God, we have a model on earth: the man Jesus. We will examine this in the next two chapters that present the model of evangelical humanism.

The encounter with real Christians, who, although they remain limited and weak, have had a genuine experience of interior liberation, appears integrated in their being, humanly fulfilled, inhabited by the Presence—the encounter with such Christians can be attractive for persons who may be inclined to seek the meaning of their lives outside the church.

The Pontifical Council for Culture, under the direction of Cardinal Ravasi, recently put in place a *Court of the Gentiles*, an initiative for dialogue between believers and nonbelievers. This forum, which holds meetings in a variety of European cities, is intended to construct a space for dialogue "with those to whom religion is something foreign, to whom God is unknown and who nevertheless do not want to be left merely Godless, but rather to draw near to him, albeit as the Unknown."[27]

At Lystra and at Athens, Paul addressed people who had no notion of the revelation of God in the Bible. Today we have to be aware of the image many people in our secularized societies have of God, of the Christian God, and especially when we are dealing with those considered "distant" from Christian faith. We need to be conscious of this image and eventually correct it.

Evangelizing is not the same thing as convincing people in an intellectual way. Evangelizing is not about proving something but about making the message desirable. The example of Paul at Lystra and at Athens invites us to propose a message about religion and spirituality emphasizing desire more than duty. Duty is imposed from outside. Desire is something coming from within.

Conclusion: From the Acts of the Apostles to the Gospel

Bearing witness to what God? The approach Paul takes at Athens is a starting point for coming to know God. It needs to be followed by another approach, specifically, the "Johannine" approach. We need to help people come to discover gradually that "God is Love" (1 John 4:8, 16).

It is in coming to know Jesus that we can know that God is Love (John 14:9). In fact, how can we really know God as he is? In order to make himself known, God took on human likeness. He was incarnated. It is in the person and the life of Jesus in the gospels that we can know God. The path that leads to him is what I call the evangelical way. The entire life of Jesus in the gospels, together with the humanist vision he presents in his words, bears witness to a God who is Love. This will be the subject of our next two chapters.[28]

We need to note that the two worlds the apostles addressed, first the Jews and then the pagan nations, were religious. They believed in divinity. They were not secularized. These missionary discourses are perhaps not the first models that a disciple of Jesus is called to use in bearing witness to the faith in our time. Here and now, should we not start with what is human? A secularized person might not be drawn to an image of God the all-powerful creator. The representation of God that such a person is willing to believe in should be desirable. The God of love and compassion that Jesus bears witness to in the gospels may well correspond to such a person's deepest desires, especially if, at the same time, this God is presented together with a positive model of humanity that appeals to his or her best hopes.

Chapter 4

The Evangelical Model
of Humanism, Part One
Jesus: A Man of Compassion

I n the secularized West, many people do not pose the question of life after death (the kerygmatic model) or the question of the existence of God (the model of Athens). On the other hand, they are in search of quality of human life in the present. According to recent surveys, two great Christians, Abbé Pierre and Sister Emmanuelle, are at the top of the list of the people most admired in France.[1]

The humanist approach is the one followed by Jesus during his public life, both with his disciples and on a larger scale with everyone who heard his words and saw his deeds. These people were invited, by the very fact of encountering him, to take a position with regard to Jesus—to become his disciple or not.

This approach, where Jesus appears as the perfect model of what it means to be human, complements the kerygmatic approach where Jesus is presented as Lord and Christ. Here, when presenting the man Jesus, it is a question of bearing witness to the exemplary quality of his life on earth and the program of life and happiness that he proposes. We are to see the witness to Jesus in the gospels and the testimony about him in the Acts of the Apostles as complementary, as the literary and theological unity of the two books Luke has given us invites us to do.

The preaching of the early Church was centered on the proclamation of Jesus Christ, with whom the kingdom was identified. Now, as then, there is a need to unite *the proclamation of the kingdom of God* (the content of Jesus' own "kerygma") and *the proclamation of the Christ-event* (the "kerygma" of the apostles). The two proclamations are complementary; each throws light on the other.[2]

During his earthly life Jesus, by his words, his actions, and his whole being, proclaimed the coming of the kingdom of God. The establishment of this kingdom is his life's work, his mission, as he affirms at the beginning of his public ministry when he says that he "came to Galilee proclaiming the Gospel of God: 'This is the time of fulfillment. The kingdom of God is at hand. Repent, and believe in the gospel'" (Mark 1:15). We might also cite the Gospel of Luke: "To the other towns also I must proclaim the good news of the kingdom of God, because for this purpose I have been sent" (Luke 4:43).

Jesus never gave a definition of the kingdom that he had come to establish. This is not the place to analyze the gospel texts that present the teaching of Jesus about the kingdom of God. The theme of the kingdom spans the extent of the gospels and it is taken up by St. Paul in several of his letters. For our purposes, we will say this much: in its deepest reality, the kingdom can be defined as the communion of all human beings with God and with each other, and this reality is made possible in the risen Jesus. To say "communion" is to say "love." The fundamental revelation of Jesus, by his entire being and his entire life, is that of a God of Love.[3] And he revealed this first of all not by his words, but by the testimony of his human life on earth, a life that was always motivated by love.

When speaking of the evangelical model, we also mean the approach Jesus took with those who became his disciples. This approach is presented in the synoptic gospels (Matthew, Mark, Luke), where we see Jesus' teaching method in his mission.[4] It is at the end of a long journey, a long road travelled with Jesus, that the disciples who remained faithful to him came to believe in him as Christ and Lord.[5] They reached that moment gradually and even painfully. In the beginning they put their trust in the man Jesus. They were struck by the exceptional quality of his humanity, especially by his compassion for people who were suffering. Then they saw in him a "rabbi," a wise man. Later still, they recognized him as a prophet, that is, they realized that his person and his words were God-bearing. Then the question was posed—and it is at the center of the three synoptic gospels: "Is he the Messiah, that is, the long-awaited liberator?"[6] As we know, the disciples' vision of the Messiah needed to be purified and deepened. It is only after the resurrection of Jesus that they were going to recognize him as Messiah and Son of God.

Reading and meditating on the gospels in their entirety allows us to understand better the humanist vision of Jesus. Obviously, this is not the place to analyze each of the gospels. In this chapter, we plan to give an overview of the Gospel of Luke, starting with some passages that help us to grasp the major qualities of the humanity of Jesus. Then, in the next chapter we will meditate on a very important passage of the Gospel of Matthew that can be considered a condensed expression of the humanist vision of Jesus for every human being: the Beatitudes.

Our brief analysis of some chosen passages is meant to invite readers to meditate on other passages of the gospels—some of these will be suggested in footnotes—in order to understand better the humanity of Jesus and his humanist project.

The Inauguration of Jesus' Ministry (Luke 4:16-21)

In Luke's gospel, Jesus begins his ministry in the synagogue of his home town of Nazareth. The event is recounted just after the account of his baptism, which he received from John, and his sojourn in the desert in preparation for his mission. The fourth chapter of this gospel tells the story in the following way:

¹⁶He came to Nazareth, where he had been brought up, and went into the synagogue on the Sabbath day as he usually did. ¹⁷He stood up to read, and they handed him the scroll of the prophet Isaiah. Unrolling the scroll he found the place where it is written:

¹⁸The Spirit of the Lord has been given to me, for he has anointed me. He has sent me to bring the good news to the poor, to proclaim liberty to captives, and to the blind new sight, to set the downtrodden free, ¹⁹to proclaim the Lord's year of favor.

²⁰He then rolled up the scroll, gave it back to the assistant and sat down. And all the eyes in the synagogue were fixed on him. ²¹Then he began to speak to them, "This text is being fulfilled today, even as you listen."

This homily of Jesus (v. 21) is undoubtedly the shortest one ever delivered! In one brief sentence Jesus states that he has come to accomplish the announcement of Isaiah the prophet: "This text is being fulfilled today." We know how this story continues. The people in his village are not interested in his commentary on the text of Isaiah and he is forced to leave his village and move on to begin his mission at Capernaum.

Note that Jesus defines his mission as accomplishment of the announcement by Isaiah concerning the arrival of a Messiah ("anointed with the Spirit," v. 18), one who bears Good News to those who suffer various forms of poverty: the "captives," the "blind," the "downtrodden."

How does Jesus accomplish this proclamation of Isaiah? His whole life will manifest it. The "today" he speaks about is in fact the entire time of his earthly mission.

After the event in Nazareth, Jesus begins to accomplish the promise of Isaiah. He goes to Capernaum, where he teaches and works healings. This attracts the curiosity of the crowds (Luke 4:42). He sees that they do not understand the meaning of his actions of healing. The rest of the gospel shows us Jesus working miracles for individuals, but first he wants to see signs of faith, that is, he wants them to see that the healing is a sign of the kingdom of God. He moves on from Capernaum rapidly, saying, "I must proclaim the Good News of the kingdom of God to the other towns too, because that is what I was sent to do" (Luke 4:43).[7]

What is implied by the proclamation of the Good News to the poor, which for Jesus is linked to the coming of the kingdom of God? The Beatitudes add some clarity to this point.

The Beatitudes in the Gospel of Luke (Luke 6:20-23)

According to the Gospel of Luke, Jesus pronounces the famous discourse on the Beatitudes rather early in his ministry. He begins by indicating who the poor are and what will be their new situation in the kingdom. Luke underlines the importance of this discourse when he writes that Jesus delivered it before "a great crowd of his disciples and a large number of the people" (Luke 6:17):

> [20]And raising his eyes toward his disciples he said: "Blessed are you who are poor, for the kingdom of God is yours. [21]Blessed are you who are now hungry, for you will be satisfied. Blessed are you who are now weeping, for you will laugh. [22]Blessed are you when people hate you, and when they exclude and insult you, and denounce your name as evil on account of the Son of Man. [23]Rejoice and leap for joy on that day! Behold, your reward will be great in heaven. For their ancestors treated the prophets in the same way."

Who are the poor in the first Beatitude? The three other Beatitudes specify them: they are the persons who are lacking in financial resources (those who are "hungry"); those who suffer on an affective level (those who "weep"); and those who suffer marginalization on a social level (those who are "hated, driven out, denounced").

These poor people are declared "happy." What a paradox it seems! Why are they declared happy? Because they are poor? No, the opposite is the case, as the second part of each Beatitude makes clear: "You are hungry now . . . you shall be satisfied; you weep now . . . you will laugh; you are rejected now . . . you will be fully integrated into the kingdom and recognized as such with its gradual arrival." Their reward is "great in heaven," that is, such as God (the Father in heaven) wants for them with the establishment of the kingdom of God. And this is already taking place on earth for Jesus and for the people who become his disciples. Happy are these poor because God draws near to them and they will no longer be poor with the coming of the kingdom. Jesus is working, first of all, to establish on earth this kingdom of "communion among all human beings." By his words and the example of his life, he is inviting those who become his disciples to be actively engaged in assuring respect, social recognition, and the establishment of just conditions for those who are poor in all senses of that word. This is an integral part of the kingdom of God that he came to inaugurate in our world.[8]

If the kingdom of justice is first of all God's work, it is also a human work, and it is the mission of the disciples to work for establishing it in our world, in the socio-political dimension itself.[9] We can formulate the following corollary: everyone who is at work in the world to fight against poverty in all its forms, to build a better, more just society, is already engaged in Jesus' project of constructing the kingdom of God on earth.[10]

We need to make a clarification: the "humanist" dimension in our world of the kingdom of God, which Jesus announces, does not cover the totality of his message and the witness of his life. Nonetheless, it is an essential component.

Jesus, a Man of Compassion

By paying special attention during his ministry to the neglected and rejected in his environment—the sick, the possessed, the public sinners, the tax collectors, the women—whom he restores to dignity, Jesus preaches by his actions the Beatitudes that he had proclaimed by his words. Associating with those rejected by society, he wants to show that the kingdom is for all, that the God he proclaims offers his love to all men and women, but in a special way to persons who do not have what they need on a material level in order to live or who live with great suffering or social rejection. I invite you to read the Gospel of Luke and meditate on the many passages where Jesus shows special consideration for those suffering and those in need.

Who then is Jesus? Let us sum up: Jesus is a man of compassion, a man of immense compassion. And his compassion is a reflection of the compassion of God the Father. Through his humanity, marked profoundly by compassionate love, Jesus reveals the love of God the Father for all human beings.

Luke gives us a key to a profound understanding of the message of his gospel in three stories, the central message of which is expressed by the use of a single Greek verb, *esplagnisthè*. In this gospel, this verb is used only in these three stories, which have no parallels in the other gospels.[11] These stories reveal the humanity of Jesus and his humanist project.

If we translate this verb literally, the Greek term *esplagnisthè* can be rendered by the expression: "He was seized in his maternal womb," i.e., the womb that engenders life. Translators often use the phrase "he was moved with pity," or "he was overcome with compassion."[12] We will comment on each of these three stories.

The Encounter with the Widow of Nain (Luke 7:11-17)

[11]Soon afterward he journeyed to a city called Nain, and his disciples and a large crowd accompanied him. [12]As he drew near to the gate of the city, a man who had died was being carried out, the only son of his mother, and she was a widow. A large crowd from the city was with her. [13]When

the Lord saw her, he was moved with pity for her and said to her, "Do not weep." ¹⁴He stepped forward and touched the coffin; at this the bearers halted, and he said, "Young man, I tell you, arise!" ¹⁵The dead man sat up and began to speak, and Jesus gave him to his mother. ¹⁶Fear seized them all, and they glorified God, exclaiming, "A great prophet has arisen in our midst," and "God has visited his people." ¹⁷This report about him spread through the whole of Judea and in all the surrounding region.

Translators generally give this episode the title, "The Resurrection of the Son of the Widow of Nain." This title expresses the principal action that takes place in the story. But we have to go deeper if we want to grasp the central message of the event described here. What is the author telling us in this text?

The situation that Jesus finds himself in is the following: a woman, a widow, loses her only son. Thus she is poor in three senses: she is a woman, she is a widow (i.e., she no longer can count on the support of her husband), and she has lost her only son (so she has lost the only support she had left). She has become one of the poorest of the poor in the Israel of that period. She has no financial resources to count on for living, except perhaps begging or prostitution. Socially marginalized, she is destined to a life of terrible solitude.

"When the Lord saw her, he was moved with compassion for her." Jesus is deeply touched by the desperate situation of this woman. What does he do to give her back her life? He "awakens her son" and "gives him back to his mother." Returning the son to life is the means he chooses to give the mother back her life.

One could say that this widow was "dead," and that Jesus has given her life once again! The central message of the account is not the resurrection of the young man, but the "resurrection" of his mother who had become one of the poorest of the poor.¹³ Here Jesus clearly announces in an action "Good News to the poor," the goal of his mission.

The Good Samaritan (Luke 10:29-37)

In this parable, Jesus broadens the horizon. He tells us how humans ought to live. But he is speaking about himself first, presenting what is implied for him to love his neighbor—to live a fulfilling human life.

> [25]There was a scholar of the Law who stood up to test him and said, "Teacher, what must I do to inherit eternal life?" [26]Jesus said to him, "What is written in the law? How do you read it?" [27]He said in reply, "You shall love the Lord, your God, with all your heart, with all your being, with all your strength and with all your mind, and your neighbor as yourself." [28]He replied to him, "you have answered correctly; do this and you will live." [29]But because he wished to justify himself, he said to Jesus, "And who is my neighbor?" [30]Jesus replied, "A man fell victim to robbers as he went down from Jerusalem to Jericho. They stripped and beat him and went off leaving him half-dead. [31]A priest happened to be going down that road, but when he saw him, he passed by on the opposite side. [32]Likewise a Levite came to the place, and when he saw him, he passed by on the opposite side. [33]But a Samaritan traveler who came upon him was moved with compassion at the sight. [34]He approached the victim, poured oil and wine over his wounds and bandaged them. Then he lifted him up on his own animal, took him to an inn and cared for him. [35]The next day he took out two silver coins and gave them to the innkeeper with the instruction. 'Take care of him. If you spend more than what I have given you, I shall repay you on my way back.' [36]Which of these three, in your opinion, was neighbor to the robbers' victim?" [37]He answered, "The one who treated him with mercy." Jesus said to him, "Go and do likewise."

We have reproduced the text of this parable of Jesus in its context, which allows us to see the originality of Jesus' teaching with regard to the Law given in the Old (or First) Testament.

When a Jewish lawyer asks Jesus what he must to do have
eternal life, Jesus responds by inviting him to repeat what is
important in the Law (the Torah). Thus he invites him to reflect
on what is essential in his religion, Judaism. This is what the
lawyer does (v. 27). But Jesus goes on to give a new interpretation of the commandment of love for one's neighbor. He "ac-
complishes" the Law given by God in the Old Testament. He
reveals it. Jesus uses a parable to present this new interpretation
in answer to the second question posed by the lawyer: "And
who is my neighbor?" At that time the question was debated
by the rabbis. The majority opinion was that the neighbor I am
supposed to love is first of all other Jews, i.e., people of the
same nation and religion. Next come the proselytes, i.e., the
foreigners who have been assimilated to the chosen people (the
gehrim). However, this duty to love did not include foreigners
in general and certainly not schismatics like the Samaritans.

Jesus does not answer the question directly. Rather he replies to another question, which is not raised, but which he
considers more important, more fundamental: what does it
mean to love? He responds by telling a parable in which there
is a sharp contrast between two attitudes regarding a man in
great distress. The priest and the Levite see the man in distress
and go out of their way to avoid him. The Samaritan sees this
man who is half dead and "is deeply moved with compassion
(*esplagnisthè*)." This heartfelt pity leads to the actions that follow. Seven steps are taken, described by seven different verbs.
He approaches, he pours oil and wine on the man's wounds,
bandages the wounds, hoists the gravely wounded man onto
his own mount, takes him to an inn, takes care of him (thus
spending time with him), and gives money to the innkeeper to
ensure that the wounded man will make a full recovery. Note
the symbolic value of these seven stages; the number "seven" is
often associated with completeness. Thus the Samaritan does
everything to bring this man fully back to life.[14] The difference
between all that the Samaritan does and the nothing that the

priest and Levite do is striking in that the Samaritan renders every possible service whereas the priest and the Levite flee at the sight of this person in distress. The response to the fundamental question "What is love for one's neighbor?" is clear: doing everything to help someone in distress.

Who loves? The answer is obvious and the lawyer has no choice but to declare it (without naming the Samaritan explicitly): "the one who treated him with mercy," i.e., the Samaritan. The lawyer's indirect manner of responding brings to light another sharp contrast in Jesus' recounting of this story. At the time of Jesus, and in fact ever since the time the Israelites returned from their exile in Babylon, they used three terms to distinguish three categories of belonging to the chosen people: priests, Levites, and the people (laypeople). Jesus' parable must have been quite surprising. No doubt, those who heard him tell the story, expected him to say, after mentioning the priest and the Levite, "a layperson came by." The appearance on the scene of the Samaritan had to be shocking. It highlights the following contrast: it is the foreigner who loves, as opposed to those who should normally give an example of love—the priest and the Levite.

Finally, we return the question posed by the lawyer. Jesus repeats the question but in an entirely different way, "reversing" the terms in which it was formulated. It is no longer: "Who is my neighbor?" but "who proved himself a neighbor . . . ?" We have passed from neighbor as object (the person that I should love—i.e., draw near to) to neighbor as subject (the person who should love—i.e., draw near to). Now the question has become: who is calling me to become a neighbor? What nearby person is suffering and needs me to draw near and offer help? To whom should I be rendering service?[15]

To love is first of all in the order of being and only then in the order of doing, of acting. Jesus goes to the very source of the action, back to what makes it happen. The question posed by the lawyer at the beginning was "What must I do?" Jesus responds at the end of the story "Go and do the same yourself." We are on the level of the ethics of doing. But between the question posed by the lawyer and its answer, Jesus underlines what sets the action in motion and qualifies it. It is the interior attitude of compassion when confronted with the suffering of another person: "He saw and he was moved with compassion." When the lawyer poses his question, Jesus sends him back to reflect on the Law's prescription "you shall love," not in order to decide what you must do but rather to answer the question "Who are you?" "Who are you in the presence of those around you who are in distress?" "Are you someone's neighbor?"

If we meditate on this parable as disciples of Jesus, we can see that it goes still deeper. Within the larger context of the Gospel, and in particular the two other stories whose central message is articulated by the verb *esplagnisthè* (moved with compassion)—Jesus and the widow of Nain in Luke 7 and the Prodigal Father in Luke 15—we are led to conclude that the one who represents the Good Samaritan is Jesus himself, not the disciples of Jesus. He alone does all, gives all in order to heal suffering persons. The disciples of Jesus enter into a process by which they gradually become Good Samaritans for those around them who are suffering.[16]

The Prodigal Father (Luke 15:11-32)

The third and final use of the Greek verb *esplagnisthè* (moved with compassion) is found in the parable usually called "The Prodigal Son." I will not reproduce here the text of this well-known parable, but I do want to invite the reader to read it and meditate on it. For our purposes I want to present two keys to open up the central message of the story.[17]

Let us look first at the context of the parable. The beginning of chapter 15 in Luke's gospel mentions the situation that led Jesus to tell this parable. "The tax collectors and sinners were all drawing near to listen to him, but the Pharisees and scribes began to complain, saying, 'This man welcomes sinners and eats with them.'" The situation is clear. Jesus receives tax collectors, who were shunned, and public sinners, i.e., people who were not faithful to the Law. He goes so far as to take meals with these "unclean" people. The use of the present tense of these verbs indicates that this was habitual behavior on the part of Jesus. The Pharisees and the scribes—the good people!—protested. Then Jesus goes on to tell three parables to justify his taking the part of the outcasts and public sinners. The third one, by far the most extensively developed of the three, reveals the profound motivation of Jesus' behavior. He acts in this way because God the Father behaves with humans in this way. The situation already indicates clearly to us that the father is the principal person in the parable, not the prodigal son or the elder son.

We will look next at the father's motivation for his actions. It is given to us in verse 20: "So he [the prodigal son] got up and went back to his father. While he was still a long way off, his father caught sight of him and was filled with compassion [*esplagnisthè*]." This new key for our reading also indicates that the father is the main character in the story. We recognize that Jesus is a being of compassion because God the Father, to whom he bears witness, is also a being of compassion, of immense compassion. What does it mean for God to be a loving Father, full of compassion for all human beings (his sons and daughters)? I would include the following elements of this love of the Father and I would invite the reader to meditate on the verses of Scripture that I have attached to these components.

For God to be a loving Father includes:

- respecting the liberty of his sons and daughters (Luke 15:12, 13, 28, 32)
- staying in place and awaiting the arrival of the one who has gone far away (v. 20)
- looking with tenderness and compassion (v. 20)

- running ahead to welcome the one who is returning (v. 20)
- forgiving without conditions (v. 20)
- rejoicing at the return and organizing a celebration (vv. 22, 23, 25)
- being gentle but firm with the one who condemns and refuses to forgive (vv. 28-32).

This parable could be called: "The father who is prodigal with the gift of forgiveness."

It is important to consider the considerable impact of this parable in the context in which it was spoken. Jesus has the "audacity" to act not only in the name of God but "like God." He, who was neither a sinner nor an outcast, broke through the established barriers and gave a warning to his hearers! Undoubtedly this was shocking to the "right-minded" people. But what we have to notice most of all is the liberating effect of such actions for those with whom he was associating. By eating with sinners and outcasts of all sorts, Jesus acknowledged them as his friends. He freed them from their frustration and from their shame. He appreciated them. He showed them that they counted as persons. Because Jesus was recognized as a man of God, his gestures of friendship, such as his welcoming and sharing meals with them, took on a religious significance (Luke 7:16; 9:19; 13:33; 24:19). Through Jesus it is God himself who welcomed these poor people. In fact, as we saw in the parable from chapter 15, Jesus himself takes responsibility for giving meaning to these actions: if he has compassion and expresses friendship for society's outcasts, it is because God the Father has compassion and friendship for them. Through his tender human gestures, Jesus reveals the tenderness of God the Father for all humans, especially the most marginal and excluded. What a great model for mission in our world today![18]

These three passages in Luke's gospel express the motivation behind the being and the deeds of Jesus. To be a disciple of Jesus is thus "to be moved to the depths of one's being" when confronted with the misery of another, as Jesus, like the Samaritan, was moved, as the prodigal father, who represents God, was moved.

For the objective of the present volume, which is evangelization in the world today, we come to the following conclusion: the disciple of Jesus Christ today bears witness to him and to the God who dwells in him. The disciple manifests for those who are suffering the kind of compassion that was present in Jesus at the moment of his encounter with the widow of Nain, the compassion that was present in the Samaritan for the man left half dead, the compassion that was present in the father of the prodigal son.

This presentation does not cover all aspects of the mission of Jesus.[19] But it seems important to highlight this "humanitarian" dimension of the kingdom, too little presented in the past. It touches the humanist quest that many today think they cannot find in a commitment to Christian life.

This humanist vision of Jesus is encapsulated in another way by the evangelist John who recounts Jesus' invitation to his disciples to "Love one another as I love you" (John 15:12; see also John 13:34). The theme comes up again in the first letter of John. After Jesus has returned to the Father his disciples come to the profound realization that "God is Love" (1 John 4:8, 16). Accordingly, the communion that God wants to establish with humans is all about love. It is only in response to God's love—by loving our brothers and sisters—that we come to really know God, to encounter God.

Christianity, a Way of Humanism

This way of looking at Jesus and his project leads me first of all to pose a double question about the mission today: how can we explain the fact that a number of those baptized in the Christian churches in the West have left their faith and have adopted an "Oriental" religion, specifically Buddhism, saying that they have found there a "religion of compassion"? And, how was the Christian religion, in which they were raised, presented to them?

If the disciples who remained faithful to Jesus had not encountered in him a man of exceptional human qualities, could they have followed him to the end? He certainly did not correspond to their expectations of a political messiah. Could they have believed in him as the Messiah after his resurrection?

How can we announce that Jesus is Christ and Lord if we do not bear witness that in this world he was a man, fully human in the sense that, in exercising his freedom, he always opted for whatever would promote communion among human beings? Thus he proclaimed a kingdom of love, of justice, and of peace.

We should recognize that, in presenting Jesus in the past, the churches have often passed over in silence this dimension of Jesus. He was a being with freedom like us, and a human being of an exceptional quality, who is a model for us, in some way "drawing us forward" in the mission of our humanity.

The terms used to present this exemplary humanity of Jesus, together with his role as Messiah and his divinity, will vary according to the times and places where we speak of him. An example: at the synod of the bishops of Asia that was held in Rome, it was strongly affirmed that "God's offer of salvation is not a set of doctrines," but rather "it is the person of Jesus himself."[20] The apostolic exhortation *Ecclesia in Asia*, which appeared in 1999, clarifies this point, saying that we should present our doctrinal position gradually and begin with images that are both faithful to the Scriptures and meaningful for the Asian mentality and cultures. Among these the exhortation mentions: "Jesus Christ as the Master of Wisdom, the Healer, the Liberator, the Spiritual Guide, the Enlightened One, the Compassionate Friend of the Poor, the Good Samaritan. Jesus can be presented as the incarnate Wisdom of God, whose grace brings forth fruit from the seeds of divine wisdom already present in the life, the religions, and the peoples of Asia" (20).

We can also see that this approach, starting with the person of Jesus, can reach peoples and cultures that remain deeply religious, as is often the case with the peoples and cultures of the Asian continent. This being said, it seems to me that this is the most appropriate approach to take in the secularized world that is mine. In this world, everything is centered on the human person and earthly realities. A "secularized" person will find our message attractive if he or she begins to perceive that Christianity is a form of humanism, a way that permits people to become fully human.[21] It is a question of helping people to see that it is in coming to know Jesus Christ that we learn what "being human" really signifies and what it means to love because all men and women are in search of true love. The Gospel needs to be heard by people today as "Good News."

Evangelizing by the Witness of One's Life

All disciples of Jesus are called, in spite of their personal limitations and fragility, to live out a compassionate love. In his 1975 apostolic exhortation, *Evangelii Nuntiandi*, Pope Paul VI wrote this sentence which still rings true: "Modern man listens more willingly to witnesses than to teachers, and if he does listen to teachers, it is because they are witnesses" (41).

Isn't evangelizing, first of all, performing acts of compassion the way Jesus did and, eventually, at an opportune moment, speaking a word that opens the way to knowing the One who is at the source of our options concerning life, Jesus Christ and God his Father who is also our Father?

Isn't evangelizing helping people discover in Jesus someone with such a quality of being and of life that others will find themselves saying: "Master, to whom shall we go? You have the words of eternal life" (John 6:68). As for the first disciples, does it not seem normal, and even desirable, that people encounter Jesus first in his humanity?

Everyone who manifests compassion upon encountering a person in distress, as Jesus and the Samaritan did (Luke 5, 10), behaves like a son or daughter of the God to whom Jesus Christ bore witness by his words and life. Such a person has a proper place within the kingdom of God. This is the way a disciple of Jesus is invited to look upon others, regardless of her or his ties with the ecclesial community. However, the disciple is convinced that it is a grace to know Jesus Christ, to be nourished with his Gospel and to be in a relationship of faith with God his Father, a grace that is an enormous support for growing in humanness.

It is in really making room for others in one's life, and especially for the disenfranchised, that a person is better led to make room for The Other, who is already present in that person's life, whether he or she has discovered that presence or not. Could we not say that there is already in such a person's life a certain encounter with God—even if it is not yet a conscious knowledge, i.e., a recognition of God?

What works manifest God? What signs are words of God? If God is Love and if Jesus bore witness to God through his love, then the signs of God's presence will have something to do with love. These signs will be human experiences of love given or received. Love with a capital "L" is, in effect, only known by experiences of love.[22]

But the Love that is God for us far surpasses current notions of human love. It is total and freely offered. The signs *par excellence* of God in our world are actions that can be characterized as gratuitous: acts like an unconditional acceptance of every person, acts like recognizing the value of another person, acts of forgiveness. Such actions pose or raise the question: "Who is behind it?"[23]

Humanism and Spirituality

Obviously, Jesus' mission does not have only a humanist dimension. Jesus was well integrated into the religious world of Judaism of his time. He bore witness to his faith in the God of Israel and to his faith in the Scriptures. He withdrew in solitude to pray. He followed the religious practices of his people by, among other things, frequenting the synagogue and the temple and celebrating the Jewish feasts. The cultural world of his time was at the same time religious. But, for Jesus, faith in the God of Israel expresses a new humanism, a new society, one that shows respect for all humans, offers justice for all, provides support for the fragile and for those suffering from all forms of poverty. It is this new humanism brought by Jesus that our secularized world needs to hear us speak about and that the disciple of Jesus is called to announce in deeds and words. This humanism brings with it an image of God: a God of justice, of compassion, of love.

Twenty years ago I was invited to give a conference on "The New Age and Christian Faith." This led me to read many publications on the New Age movement. This movement defined itself as a spirituality, and asserted that such was not the case for Christian religions. In this gallery of the New Age, many groups presented themselves as paths for human growth, as "humanism." Why is it that the search for spirituality and humanism is carried out elsewhere and not in the Christian churches? The Gospel is a great book of spirituality and humanism, and the two dimensions are closely linked. Human growth and spiritual growth go together.

Nonetheless, it is important to note a fundamental difference between Christian spirituality and the spiritualities of the New Age. For a Christian, God is Someone, a Person distinct from myself, although God is not far from me. In the New Age, God is confused with the cosmos and the human world. In fact, it is more a religion of the divine than a religion of God. In the end these spiritualities leave us to ourselves, to our own powers, in order to liberate us. As opposed to that, the Gospel of Jesus is truly Good News: there is a personal God, who intervenes in order to liberate us completely, despite our fragility and our incapacity. The great program of humanization, of liberation to which we aspire, is ultimately a gift of God.

The Commitment to Social Justice

Among the various paths that lead us to encounter Jesus Christ and the God he reveals, some choose the way that involves social commitment: the way of love for others that is expressed in defending the marginalized and the exploited in our society as well as those who suffer from poverty in its many forms.

When the church is engaged in various ways with organizations that offer economic and social assistance (justice, peace, the integrity of creation), it bears witness and serves the mission of evangelization. And every Christian who gets involved in what are called "humanitarian acts" is also a sign of the kingdom.

Contemporary Invitations

In our witnessing to the Gospel, the church invites us to start with what people are experiencing. The Second Vatican Council's pastoral constitution on the church in the modern world (*Gaudium et Spes*) begins with this affirmation: "The joys and hopes, the griefs and anguish of the people of our time, especially of those who are poor or afflicted, are the joys and hopes, the grief and anguish of the followers of Christ as well. Nothing that is genuinely human fails to find an echo in their hearts" (1).

In the apostolic exhortation published after the completion of the last synod on the Word of God, Benedict XVI wrote: "Jesus himself says that he came that we might have life in abundance (John 10:10). Consequently, we need to make every effort to share the word of God as an openness to our problems, a response to our questions, a broadening of our values and the fulfillment of our aspirations" (*Verbum Domini* 23).

Of Gods and Men, a film about the monks martyred at Tibhirine, has been enormously successful with the public worldwide. Why does this film touch the hearts of so many people? It presents a group of men of faith, who have given themselves over entirely to God, as people who are very human, very honest, and faithful in their dealings with each other and with the Muslim villagers they serve without ever converting them. This film gave Christians a good opportunity to speak about their faith.

Etymologically, as we know, the word "Gospel," means "Good News," and it does us good to hear this message.

Chapter 5

The Evangelical Model of Humanism, Part Two
The Way to Happiness

We will now look at another evangelical humanist approach that is complementary to the one we have just seen, in which Jesus is a model of what it means to be human because of his exemplary compassion. In Matthew's gospel, we find a text of the Beatitudes formulated in a way that is different from its articulation in the Gospel of Luke. In the context of Matthew's gospel, we can consider this announcement of the Beatitudes as a condensed form of Jesus' humanist agenda, addressed to people who will respond to his call to become his disciples. St. Augustine, who was the first author to compose a commentary on the Sermon on the Mount, wrote at the beginning of his considerable work that Jesus' discourse is "the charter document of the Christian life."[1] Commenting on the Beatitudes that open the Sermon on the Mount, he considers them a summary of the entire discourse (Matt 5:3-12). Given the fact that Jesus' declaration "happy" ["blessed"] is repeated eight times in this brief passage and is applied to those who live by what follows that word each time it appears, we can define the Beatitudes as the Way to Happiness proposed by Jesus.

It is generally recognized that Luke wrote his gospel and the Acts of the Apostles for non-Jewish people of Greek culture who had become Christians. Matthew's gospel, on the other hand, was addressed to Jewish Christians. Even if Matthew and Luke draw on the same sources, coming from the same tradition, and both of them write in Greek, the accounts of the discourse in Matthew contain elements that are found only in his text and that are expressed in different terms, with more expressions and references coming from the Old (First) Testament.[2]

The Beatitudes in the Gospel according to Matthew (Matt 5:3-10)

> [1]When he saw the crowds, he went up the mountain, and after he had sat down, his disciples came to him. [2]He began to teach them, saying: [3]"Blessed are the poor in spirit, for theirs is the kingdom of heaven. [4]Blessed are they who mourn, for they will be comforted. [5]Blessed are the meek, for they will inherit the land. [6]Blessed are they who hunger and thirst for righteousness, for they will be satisfied. [7]Blessed are the merciful, for they will be shown mercy. [8]Blessed are the clean of heart, for they will see God. [9]Blessed are the peacemakers, for they will be called children of God. [10]Blessed are they who are persecuted for the sake of righteousness, for theirs is the kingdom of heaven.

These Beatitudes can be easily committed to memory.[3] The first one and the last one use the same terms to describe the promised reward: "For theirs is the kingdom of heaven." The eighth one takes up again the theme of the fourth on "justice" (NABRE: "righteousness"), but with a particular qualification: "persecuted for justice."[4]

The text of the Beatitudes in the Gospel of Matthew is one of the most difficult passages in the Bible to understand, because the meaning of each Beatitude is not specified. Spontaneously, we project on the words the meaning that they have in our language and culture. For example, we might assume that the "meek" are people who do not get angry easily and that those who "hunger and thirst for justice" are those who fight for social justice.

I spent several years doing research on the Sermon on the Mount, and I wrote several works on "this first and most powerful discourse of Jesus" (according to the great French seventeenth-century preacher, Bishop Bossuet). Here I would like to outline briefly the conclusions I came to with regard to the meaning of each of the Beatitudes. If readers want to know more about how I reached these conclusions, I would refer them to two works I published as the fruit of my study.[5]

Since we have already examined in the previous chapter of this work the Beatitudes in the Gospel of Luke, I would like to anticipate a conclusion that can help to guide the reader through the analysis that will follow: whereas the Beatitudes in Luke present the dimension of social engagement of the kingdom, those in Matthew convey its ethical and spiritual dimensions.

A Declaration about Happiness

Before presenting the meaning of each Beatitude, I need to offer some explanations of other elements in the text.

- "Blessed" or "Happy." The Greek word *makarios* that Matthew uses is the translation of the Hebrew term *ashré*, which appears 45 times in the Hebrew Scriptures, mainly in the Psalms (25 times) and the Wisdom literature. The "macarism," i.e., the Beatitude, is a form of congratulations (Bravo to you!). When Jesus says "Blessed are you," he is proclaiming the happiness of the person who fits the description found in the Beatitude.

- *Are* happy *or will be* happy? The first part of the Beatitudes does not contain a verb. In Greek, therefore, the meaning must be present and not future. The Beatitude is not a promise of happiness for the future (in heaven!) but a declaration of happiness in the present.

- How can we understand this affirmation as referring to happiness in the present? The second part of each Beatitude, introduced by "for," provides the reason for the happiness. These persons are happy because they are part of the kingdom that has already begun: "for the kingdom of heaven is theirs." The "kingdom of heaven" is a Semitic way of saying "the kingdom of God." The verbs in the second half of verses 3 and 10, which form a sort of inclusion, are in the present. But the persons are also happy by reason of the hope-filled future that is opening up before them: "for they will inherit the earth," "for they will be consoled," and so forth. The verbs are in the future in verses 4-9. These other formulations in the Beatitudes 2-7 are ways of speaking about the "kingdom of God," but with various images taken from the Old Testament and from Judaism. To say, for example, that "those who hunger and thirst for righteousness will be satisfied," or that "those with pure hearts will see God," is another way of saying that those who are living out these Beatitudes already have a foretaste of the blessings of the kingdom.

We are far from the concepts of happiness current in modern societies, that is, satisfaction of all earthly desires, absence of problems and suffering, a psychological state of euphoric happiness, or the experience of strong sensations. The happiness described by the Beatitudes is a happiness that comes to us as a gift, not a happiness we produce. It does not exclude privation or suffering. This happiness is a veritable (interior) joy that results from a state of harmony with others, with God, and with oneself.

Jesus could proclaim the Beatitudes because he was the first to live them. They reflect his experience, in his actual practice of faith and hope, passing through suffering and the shadow of the cross. Jesus, therefore, is the model and the guarantee of happy existence.

The Meaning of Each of the Beatitudes

In order to understand the significance of each Beatitude in the Gospel of Matthew, we must consider three factors: the origin of the Beatitude, that is, the meaning of the term in the Old Testament and in Judaism that inspired Jesus and the evangelists; other uses of the term in the Gospel of Matthew; and the witness given in the life of Jesus, the first to live the Beatitudes he proclaimed. Now for some notes on each of the Beatitudes:

- *The "poor in spirit."* In the background we recognize the *'anâwim* ("stooped") of the Old Testament and the Jewish writings of Qumrân. The *'anâwim* are those who are socially oppressed, obliged to stoop or bend forward before the rich and powerful. In the Psalms and the prophetic books, the term designates the attitude of a person prostrate before God and waiting for his help. Thus, the "poor in spirit" are people who bend down inwardly, submitting themselves totally to God and drawing their strength from him. These are humble people, as most of the fathers of the church understood them. We already live this Beatitude when we recognize that all the earthly ways of filling up our lives (possessions, power, and prestige) are an illusion; they cannot really satisfy our longings. We glimpse this Beatitude when we acknowledge the emptiness within and do not try to camouflage it.

- *"The meek."* The Old Testament background and the Matthean context indicate that this Beatitude has essentially the same meaning as the one concerning the "poor in spirit." In fact, it is directly inspired by Psalm 37:11, from which it takes the Greek words: "the meek shall inherit the earth." In the Greek version (known as the *Septuagint*) of this psalm, the Greek word *praeis* translates the Hebrew word *'anâwim*, which is the background of the first Beatitude. This Beatitude adds an element to the first one. The "meek" remain patient in waiting and do not seek to do violence to God, or to grasp from him what they desire. This attitude contrasts with the attitude behind the pagan's prayer in Matthew 6:7-8. Jesus is the model for both of these two Beatitudes: "Learn from me, for I am meek and humble of heart" (Matt 11:29).

- *"They who mourn" (the "afflicted").* This Beatitude is the only one that has an equivalent in the text of Luke ("Blessed are you who are now weeping"; Luke 6:21). The source text is from Isaiah 61:2, "comfort all who mourn." The Greek word *penthos* designates very intense suffering. In the context of the two Beatitudes that precede it (vv. 3-4) and the one that follows it (v. 6), which indicate an attitude with regard to God, the Beatitude about the afflicted involves an ethical and religious sense. It concerns persons who live with great human suffering with an attitude of confidence in God.

- *"They who hunger and thirst for righteousness."* The term "righteousness" is an important one in the Sermon on the Mount, where it introduces new developments three times (Matt 5:20; 6:1, 33). In these passages, "justice" designates a human act in conformity with what God wants. It is about being "adjusted" to God. To hunger and thirst for justice is, therefore, to desire ardently and to strive actively to live according to the will of God, as Jesus teaches, and to do this despite the persecutions that the disciple will undergo (vv. 10-12; see also 10:17-25).

- *"The merciful."* In the Old Testament, mercy, which is rarely attributed to a human being, has two essential aspects: the divine forgiveness of faults and the active benevolence God shows for persons in need. A single Hebrew term designates the womb and mercy; it comes from *rehem*, the uterus, the maternal womb, as we observed in the last chapter. To be merciful is to be "seized in the womb," to be "overcome with compassion" when confronted with a situation of great suffering or misery. The context of the Gospel of Matthew indicates two ways of practicing this Beatitude, coming to the aid of all suffering misery, as the famous text of the last judgment calls us to do (Matt 25:31-46), and forgiving. The parable of the unforgiving debtor (Matt 18:23-35) shows that forgiving others follows from the forgiveness received from God.[6]

- *"The clean of heart."* The formulation of this Beatitude seems to have its origin in Psalm 24:4-6, which contains the expression "pure of heart," to describe the person who stands before God in all honesty and integrity. The Beatitude speaks of persons who have no malice, who seek what is good, who are upright and loyal to God and to their neighbor. The pure of heart are true, authentic. You can count on them. They inspire confidence.[7]

- *"The peacemakers."* Against the Old Testament background (where the Hebrew word "shālōm," which is also used to speak about the salvation of the messianic times, signifies "peace,"), the peacemakers are those who work to reconcile humans who are divided (Matt 5:23-24). On a larger scale, they are persons who work to establish favorable conditions so that individuals and peoples can flourish in all the dimensions of their humanity.

The first three Beatitudes turn us toward God: they invite us to be open to him in order to find fulfillment. The fourth moves us from openness to God to openness to others, since the thirst for living according to the will of God includes both dimensions. The Beatitudes of the merciful, the pure of heart, and the peacemakers teach us to develop just behavior toward our brothers and sisters in the human family. Thus, the kind of Christian ethic proposed in the Beatitudes is rooted in spirituality.

The Beatitudes are points of entry into the kingdom because they are concrete ways of loving: love of God and of neighbor, communion with God (the first four) and with others (the following four). This is a lifelong project. But living one Beatitude already places us within the kingdom.[8] Evangelizing is helping people find their door into the kingdom, their Beatitude.

Even though each of the Beatitudes has a meaning and content proper to itself, they cannot be separated. They are like chords in a harmonious symphony.

The disciples of Jesus are witnesses of a spiritual humanism where openness to others and to God go together. They bear witness that being open to God opens us to others, and even more, motivates and nourishes humanism, relating with others.

"Blessed" without Knowing It

At the heart of his mission, Jesus proclaims: "Blessed . . . Blessed." The Beatitudes of the Gospel present a program for success in life: that which gives happiness and meaning to human existence.[9] Everyone wants to be happy! Jesus, the wise man, invites his disciple, by his words, and more fundamentally by his being, to accept and present the Gospel as the path to happiness.[10] This presupposes that disciples take the Beatitudes as the project of their lives, even if they live them imperfectly.

Nonetheless, many today see themselves "outside of" the church, of Christian faith, of the Gospel. Christian witnesses, evangelizers, have another view of them. They are already living, in varying degrees, one or another Beatitude from Matthew's gospel, at least in some circumstances of their lives. And so they are "within" the kingdom. They are within the kingdom when they are generous, merciful, peacemakers, thirsting for authenticity ("pure of heart"). And so they should be proud of themselves. They have the feeling that they are growing in their humanity. The evangelizer can tell them that they are living the Gospel more often than they think. They have a taste for the

Gospel. They are already on the inside. They are invited to live something more, something better, as they come to know the Gospel and to know Jesus Christ. Knowledge of Jesus Christ and his Good News will enable them to be fed and nourished by what they are already living, the life of the kingdom.

To recognize persons for what they are and for what they are doing to become more human, isn't that already evangelizing? Announcing the Good News is telling persons, even non-believers, by our attitudes and eventually with our words: "You are already living the Gospel, whenever you live one or another of the Beatitudes. Don't you want to know it better? Don't you want to know the one who proclaimed it and bore witness to it by his entire life? Doesn't that make you want to be fed at the source, Jesus Christ who is alive and with us in his Spirit?

It seems to me that, in the end, evangelizing is saying to someone: you are beautiful because you are in the image of God! The mission of evangelizing is awakening people to what is the best in them, awakening them to their deepest desire, their deep thirst to love and be loved.

The evangelizer ought to express in actions and in words that Jesus' project, as it is summed up in the Beatitudes and the Sermon on the Mount (Matt 5–7), is not governed by exterior commandments. It is first of all a lifelong project and the disciple never reaches the point where this project is complete. Once we commit ourselves to this project, we are never finished growing in our humanity.

The mission of the church is to work for the coming of the kingdom, even beyond its boundaries. Shouldn't it announce this Good News to people of all outlooks who are living by the values of the Beatitudes? Bravo! You are on the way to the kingdom. You are already living by its values. Keep going! Like those "admitted to the kingdom" in the famous passage of Matthew's gospel (Matt 25:31-46), many will undoubtedly be amazed to hear that they are living the Gospel values, that they are directing their actions according to the teaching of Jesus, that they are "within," when they thought they were "outside." Then perhaps they will have a taste for knowing more about the Gospel, about Jesus and about the community of those who are committed to following him. Perhaps they will really want to join with others in celebrating these values that are present within them together with the One who is the source of these values.

In the Beatitudes, Jesus makes clear that the kingdom of God is present where people are living in transparency of heart, working to relieve misery, actively engaged in the pursuit of peace (Matt 5:7-9). And so the kingdom of God is being built, that is to say God is at the heart of these situations that capture the best of humanity. The kingdom of God takes up and assumes human efforts of love, justice, peace, and life. In the Gospel, revealing the divinity of God means at the same time realizing the humanity of the human race. Thus, it is in situations of humanizing that we have the best possibilities of having a spiritual experience, an experience of the Christian God. We are not less Christian because we are more human, quite the contrary!

The offer of the God of Jesus Christ is in the line of a plus for our humanity, not a gap in our humanity that needs to be filled. Rather, after the first gift of creation, this is a new gift that God offers us, as an increase to our humanity. In offering each human person a covenant of love, God wants to be the partner in a mutually chosen encounter.

Life's Project for Everyone

We return now to the Gospel of Matthew. At the beginning of the Sermon on the Mount, Jesus seems to address his teaching only to his disciples, but "the crowds" are in the background (Matt 5:1-2). At the end of his discourse, it is said that "The crowds were astonished at his teaching, for he taught them as one having authority, and not as their scribes" (Matt 7:28-29). Thus, Jesus' teaching in the Sermon on the Mount should be the explicit rule of life for his disciples, that is, for Christians, but it is equally intended to enlighten and guide every person in every place and in every time. However, this will happen through the disciples' proclamation of it (Matt 28:19-20) and especially by the witness of their lives: "You are the salt of the earth. . . . You are the light of the world" (Matt 5:13-16). If you live by the Beatitudes, the world will hear and take to heart the invitations Jesus extends through this Sermon.[11]

The church has received the secret of happiness, not in order to keep it selfishly to itself, but to proclaim it to the world. The happiness of the Beatitudes is for the world, for everyone. If the lighthouse of the Beatitudes were to be extinguished, the whole world would be in darkness.

A Collective Reality

The signs of God in our world are not only individual ones but also communitarian. In the story of God's self-manifestation, He has given himself to encounter us through the witness of believing communities: in the life of the people of Israel, in the group of the first disciples who experienced the event of Pentecost, in the ecclesial communities that have gathered in the course of the centuries, right up to the present. What about today?

The kingdom of God is a collective reality. It is the project of a society that begins in the here and now, but always a society with a quality altogether different from that of our world. The most telling sign of the kingdom of God—and therefore of God—is believing communities that announce in our world a new way of living together in communion (*koinōnia*) and taking its inspiration from the model of the first church described in the Acts of the Apostles: believing communities, prayerful and loving, that present an alternative model of "society" for humanity (see Acts 2:42-47; 4:32-35).

By his words, and first of all by his life, Jesus teaches us that the love of God and the love of others grow together. Really loving others and working for their human growth and for their happiness are signs that we have taken our place within the love of God, that we receive this love, and, therefore, that we encounter God. "If anyone says, 'I love God,' but hates his brother, he is a liar; for whoever does not love a brother whom he has seen cannot love God whom he has not seen" (1 John 4:20; see also 4:8). It is the same for the encounter with Jesus Christ. The great text of Matthew 25:31-46 reminds us that one of the privileged places for this encounter is the brother or the sister who is suffering and for whom we have active compassion.[12]

In the Sermon on the Mount, Jesus even gives a new commandment to his disciples: "Love your enemies." Never in the time before Jesus was this precept articulated in such a radical and absolute manner.[13] Why love one's enemies? In order to be "sons and daughters of God, our Father," who loves everyone, "the good and the bad alike." Thus we never are Christians, rather we become Christians gradually. This is a continuing evangelization of ourselves. After meditating on the Beatitudes, the disciple of Jesus can ask: what Beatitude do I feel called to live out and express at the present time?

Conclusion: From the Gospel to the Kerygma

We will conclude these presentations on a Gospel model of evangelization with the following reflection. In presenting Jesus as a model of humanism, we are always in some way in the process of announcing the kerygma, the first model we examined, as paradoxical as that may seem at first glance. We have come full circle in the journey of faith. It is not confessing Jesus Christ and Lord, but confessing Jesus the man, Jesus the fully human one. Yet again it is confessing—in the sense of recognizing—that he is for all people uniquely, but also archetypally the model of perfect humanity.

Presenting Jesus Christ and the Christian faith as the model of perfect humanity is a first approach to evangelization. It is not all of evangelization. First evangelization will not be complete until the kerygma is announced and received, that is, when the decision to believe in Jesus as Christ and Lord will be made and celebrated in the sacrament of baptism. Evangelization, the Christian mission, cannot be reduced to the proclamation of the values of the kingdom, of human values expressed by Jesus in the Gospel and presented in the present chapter. The humanist approach is a path that must lead to kerygma, that is, to the proclamation and the reception of Jesus as Christ and Lord and of the God he reveals. Presenting Christianity merely as a form of humanism, even if it is the best kind of humanism, would mean remaining in secularity, remaining within the horizon of our world. Christian faith, in its heart, is openness to the transcendent. Evangelizing, in the end, is inviting people to welcome Jesus as Savior and to enter into the community of believers, that is, the church, in order to celebrate and nourish our faith on a regular basis with other disciples of Christ.

Let's be more precise. To be Christian is, on the one hand, to adopt the gospels as the inspiration of one's life, to choose Jesus in his earthly humanity as the model of a fully fruitful life. And, on the other hand, it is also to be able to respond to the question that Jesus addressed to his disciples during his earthly sojourn with them: "But who do you say that I am?" (Matt 16:15; Mark 8:29; Luke 9:20). The response to this question is the confession: "You are Lord and Christ,"[14] an option for faith. Jesus, then, is not simply a model of a fruitful life. He is present today in my life by his Spirit and he supports me in my option to live a fully fruitful life like his own. Then, gradually, as a baptized believer, I learn to nourish myself with his presence in prayer, in the Word, and the Eucharistic bread in order to grow in humanity, in my relationships with others, and with God. At this point we have moved beyond the object of the present book, which is evangelization in a secularized world, opening to the option of faith. Now we are in the realm of catechesis and pastoral practice, which presuppose adherence to the faith and have as their goal to lead people to maturity in faith.

Chapter 6

The Model of Emmaus

The story of Emmaus is such a wonderful tale! Luke places it at the turning point between the Gospel and the Acts of the Apostles. The risen Jesus himself is the model of the evangelizer, the missionary. In a narrative, Luke offers a brief treatise on mission, which can be adapted well to our world today.

In fact, it is not simply a story about a past event. The account of Emmaus occupies the central place of the last chapter of the Gospel of Luke, which is consecrated to recounting the resurrection of Jesus and the sending of the disciples on mission.[1] It throws light on the second volume of Luke's work, the Acts of the Apostles, which is dedicated to the mission of the disciples of Jesus in the early days of the church.[2] This text, at once simple and profound, is the result of a long development in the reflection of the first Christians in the church. It sustained their faith and their missionary enterprise.

The Story of the Apparition to the Disciples on the Road to Emmaus (Luke 24:13-35)

> [13]Now that very day two of them were going to a village seven miles from Jerusalem called Emmaus, [14]and they were conversing about all the things that had occurred. [15]And it happened that while they were conversing and debating, Jesus himself drew near and walked with them,

¹⁶but their eyes were prevented from recognizing him.
¹⁷He asked them, "What are you discussing as you walk
along?" They stopped, looking downcast. ¹⁸One of them,
named Cleopas, said to him in reply, "Are you the only
visitor to Jerusalem who does not know of the things that
have taken place there in these days?" ¹⁹And he replied to
them, "What sort of things?" They said to him, "The things
that happened to Jesus the Nazarene, who was a prophet
mighty in deed and word before God and all the people,
²⁰how our chief priests and rulers both handed him over
to a sentence of death and crucified him. ²¹But we were
hoping that he would be the one to redeem Israel; and
besides all this, it is now the third day since this took place.
²²Some women from our group, however, have astounded
us: they were at the tomb early in the morning ²³and did
not find his body; they came back and reported that they
had indeed seen a vision of angels who announced that he
was alive. ²⁴Then some of those with us went to the tomb
and found things just as the women had described, but
him they did not see." ²⁵And he said to them, "Oh, how
foolish you are! How slow of heart to believe all that the
prophets spoke! ²⁶Was it not necessary that the Messiah
should suffer these things and enter into his glory?" ²⁷Then
beginning with Moses and all the prophets, he interpreted
to them what referred to him in all the scriptures. ²⁸As
they approached the village to which they were going, he
gave the impression that he was going on farther. ²⁹But
they urged him, "Stay with us, for it is nearly evening and
the day is almost over." So he went in to stay with them.
³⁰And it happened that, while he was with them at table,
he took bread, said the blessing, broke it, and gave it to
them. ³¹With that their eyes were opened and they recognized him, but he vanished from their sight. ³²Then they
said to each other, "Were not our hearts burning (within
us) while he spoke to us on the way and opened the scriptures to us?" ³³So they set out at once and returned to
Jerusalem where they found gathered together the eleven
and those with them ³⁴who were saying, "The Lord has

truly been raised and has appeared to Simon!" [35]Then the
two recounted what had taken place on the way and how
he was made known to them in the breaking of the bread.

This account presents, in condensed form, the stages of a
complete process of evangelization, on the one hand, and on the
other a complete process of Christian commitment. First we will
look at how Jesus, the model evangelizer, goes about this task.
We will try to see how he proceeds with these two travelers who
have left the community of disciples. Think of them as people
we know who have withdrawn from the church and the practice
of the faith. They represent many people we might consider
"far off." We will see shortly the spiritual itinerary of the two
travelers: moving from their dashed hopes and their departure
from the group of disciples to their hurried return to the community where they become joyful witnesses of the risen Lord.

Jesus, the Model Evangelizer

How does Jesus go about it? What does he do first? He does
not speak. He does not try to convince. He meets the disciples
on the road of life and he listens to them. What a difference
from the vision that we often have of the witness, of the missionary! We can distinguish six stages in the missionary strategy
of Jesus in this story.

*1. He takes the initiative and approaches these travelers who have
lost all hope (vv. 13-16)*[3]

Jesus approaches them, he does not identify himself, and he
walks with them without saying anything. He listens to their
conversation. The invitation for the witness, for the evangelizer
today, who takes Jesus as his or her model, is to go meet people
where they are on the journey of their lives and listen to them
as they express their concerns, their suffering, and their disappointments.[4]

We could continue our meditation on the attitude Jesus asks of his disciples (which is the attitude we find in Jesus himself when he meets with people in distress) by contemplating the parable of the Good Samaritan from this same Gospel of Luke that we have presented in the fourth chapter of this book (Luke 10:29-37). This parable is an invitation to compassion, and more specifically an invitation to see the interior wounds, the problems, the anxieties that keep another person from living well, and an invitation to care for that person to the extent that we are able. Remember that the Good Samaritan, who figures so prominently in that story, represents Jesus. He alone does everything possible to heal those who are wounded by life. Called as we are to become at least something like the "Samaritan" for others, we remain, nonetheless, vulnerable, wounded and in need of compassion and healing.

2. Jesus asks questions . . . and listens to the answers (vv. 17-24)

At a certain moment, Jesus enters their conversation and asks a question. Actually, he poses two: "What are you discussing as you walk along?" and "What sort of things?" Jesus encourages them to say more. These are very sober questions that invite the others to express and articulate what they are experiencing, to go into more depth.[5] By questioning them, Jesus invites the travelers first to recount the events they have experienced and especially to express their deep feelings of despair (v. 21) and their feelings of being overwhelmed (v. 22).[6]

Jesus invites them to express themselves and he listens to them right to the end. He listens respectfully to what they have been through. His hearing gives the two travelers the opportunity to be gradually liberated of a weight and a sadness that has been burdening them and blinding them. Thus liberated, they can be open to the word of Jesus. Listening prepares the way for the Word! These persons who have been heard, who have been able to express themselves, are now ready to receive the word of the other.

Having come to meet them, having questioned them and having listened to them, Jesus now has their confidence and can address a word to them. The two travelers are now expecting something from their traveling companion.

The invitation is clear for the witnesses, for the evangelizers that we are called to be. This invitation is addressed to all the disciples of Jesus, and first of all to priests, who are formed to be "men of the word"—they are not always good listeners! We are invited to meet people on the pathways of their lives and to listen to them and to encourage them to speak about their preoccupations. We have to start bearing witness to the Gospel, not by speaking words but by listening attentively.[7] Listening to the person in front of him or her, the Christian disciple will learn the words and attitudes to adopt in order to meet the other person at the deepest level. It is a question of hearing about people's sufferings, but also about their expectations, their desires, and their hungers.

Listening can surprise us. It will perhaps give us the opportunity to discover a spiritual openness, and even a dimension of faith, in persons who we might spontaneously think are far from that kind of depth. Meditate on passages in the gospels that manifest Jesus' amazement at the faith of persons who in his context were not considered religious at all: his encounter with the Roman centurion (Luke 7:1-10), Zacchaeus (Luke 19:1-10), the Samaritan woman (John 4:5-42), the Canaanite woman (Matt 15:21-28).

3. Jesus speaks (vv. 25-27)

It is possible to divide what Jesus has to say in two parts. He begins by shaking up his conversation partners ("Oh, how foolish you are! How slow of heart to believe . . . .")! He has the courage to "challenge them," to "wake them up." He invites them to get beyond the narrow and selfish vision that they had revealed in expressing themselves (see v. 21). They were trying to fit Christ into the mold of a political leader in answer to their needs. Jesus makes them realize that the desires of their hearts are too limited. He can challenge them and awaken them because he had gained their confidence by listening to them.

In the second part of what he has to say, Jesus delivers the key to interpret what has happened. The travelers were blocked by the sad event they had lived through. Jesus helps them discover a meaning in the events by situating them in the larger perspective of God's plan.[8] Once again he proceeds with a question, but it is a question that includes its answer. He proposes—he does not impose—a meaning of the recent events.

The two travelers were fixated on the sad event of the death of Jesus. He helps them to enlarge their horizon and situate this event within the context of the history of salvation. He enlightens their minds and warms their hearts: "Were not our hearts burning (within us) while he spoke to us on the way . . . ?" Jesus restores their hope.

As evangelizers following the example of Jesus, we are invited to listen to people—their grievances, their suffering, and their despair—but we cannot stop there. People have the right to hear the Word of the Gospel, the Word of hope and of life, and the Good News of the Resurrection, in a language that enlightens the mind and warms the heart.

4. Jesus accepts their invitation (vv. 28-29)

This is the first moment when Jesus does not take the initiative. Up to this point, he went out of his way to meet them on the road. He invited them to speak about what was happening in their lives. And he has enlightened them.

Jesus opens the horizon of longing. He gives a meaning to what people were experiencing, but he always leaves the other person free to accept his word and his person. He proposes; he does not impose. This is the meaning of verse 28: "he made as if to go on."

Now it is the two travelers who speak up. They insist that he "stay with them." They have been encountered and moved. They want to hear more. They extend an invitation. They choose to be hospitable. This is the first step in accepting the message of Jesus, and therefore his person as well. Without this invitation, Jesus would have remained a stranger. Jesus—the evangelizer—never forces himself into the place where people live. But neither will he ever refuse an invitation!

The text says that Jesus "went in to stay with them," meaning that he went to dwell within them.[9]

From this point onward in the account of Emmaus we pass from the exterior to the interior. Moreover, the discourse will no longer be about events but the person, about the identity of the stranger who had traveled incognito with them. The meal is also a privileged place of encounter with people as they are. The passage from the exterior to the interior and the meal illustrate symbolically the transformation that is taking place in the heart of the disciples as they come to know this stranger.

5. Jesus takes the initiative once again (vv. 30-31a)[10]

Jesus has been invited by his disciples, but once he has entered the house, it is his. He becomes their host. As such, he invites them to enter into full communion with him. "He took the bread and said the blessing, broke it, and gave it to them." At this sign the former disciples recognized him: "their eyes were opened."[11] This sign is particularly significant because it comes at the end of a long process. Jesus prepared them for this peak moment, which is their recognition of who he is in the breaking of the bread. Transposing it for today, the encounter in the Eucharist becomes significant when Jesus has been encountered first of all in our personal experience and then in the Word of the Gospel.

6. "Then he vanished from their sight" (v. 31b)

Jesus does not abandon his disciples. He does not leave them. He is no longer present before them, but he dwells within them.

Jesus refuses to let himself be held back by them, to let them grasp him, to let himself be enclosed within a sign. They have recognized him in a sign and that is enough. The sign has done its work. From now on the disciples—for they have become disciples once again—will live in Jesus by faith. Jesus did not leave. "He went in to stay with them." He remains present to them, but in another way, not in his physical body.[12]

In ceasing to be visible, but remaining spiritually present to them, Jesus pushes them from inside to live no longer turned inward on themselves, but to return to the human community, to be part of the group of other believers and to bear witness (vv. 33-34).

Jesus' approach joins together two dimensions: on the one hand, solidarity, presence to people, to their experience and to their suffering; on the other hand, an awakening and enlightening, pushing people outwards, awakening them to something more, something better, followed by an enlightening through the Word. We might speak of "a pedagogy or awakening of longing."

The story of Emmaus also shows that the role of the evangelizer is not to bring God to people. God is already there. The evangelizer is called to help people perceive the presence of God who is always with them.

The story is a treatise on mission in a condensed form. It is clear that this process of accompaniment addressed to a person without hope can take months or years. In every person, the fundamental religious and moral choices take time.

On the other hand, in our secularized environments formerly considered "Catholic," there are many "nonpracticing" persons who come into contact with the church for services like the baptism of an infant, a marriage, or funerals. Isn't this an opportunity given to members of the Christian community that welcomes them—especially pastors—to listen to them (the reasons they have come, their expectations, their desires), to dialogue with them, to explain the meaning of the ritual celebration? In parishes should we not take special care with the celebration of funerals that bring together many nonbelievers or nonpracticing Catholics?

A Journey to the Encounter with Jesus Christ

It is also good to meditate on the story of Emmaus from the point of view of the two travelers who left the group of Jesus' disciples with their hopes dashed, and who in the end rush back to rejoin that group and become witnesses of the risen Lord. We can see in these two disillusioned travelers many baptized Christians who no longer go to church because they do not find any reason to be there and to live there.[13]

Note, first of all, that the transformation of these travelers is slow and laborious. This is symbolized by the image of the road. They walk (v. 13). Then they stop (v. 17). We see them on the road again (v. 28). Then they stop for dinner (v. 30). Finally they leave to return to Jerusalem (v. 33).

Alternating between continuing the journey and pausing along the way provides a good illustration of the spiritual itinerary. Faith implies a process of development! Conversion, encounter, implies movement and growth. The two travelers come to recognize the risen Jesus, to see him with the eyes of faith, little by little. Moreover, Jesus himself recognizes how hard it is for them to believe. This corresponds to our own human difficulty in coming to believe. Our coming to faith is often the product of a long journey. Learning how to be patient with ourselves is a necessary condition for being patient with the people we are called to evangelize.

In the Acts of the Apostles, the new life inaugurated in the Resurrection of Jesus bears the simple but very meaningful name of "the Way." For example, it is said that Saul the persecutor was going to Damascus to arrest the followers of the Way and that Apollos "had been instructed in the Way of the Lord . . . [but] when Priscilla and Aquila heard him, they took him aside and explained to him the Way [of God] more accurately."[14]

We can identify seven stages in the spiritual journey of the disciples on the road to Emmaus.

First attitude: They are sinking into sadness, despair,
resignation (v. 17)

When Jesus arrives and joins them on the road and asks them about the topic of their conversation, they stop, "looking downcast," and recount their woes. They had put all their hope in Jesus, this "prophet mighty in deed and word." Now he has been put to death by the religious leaders. The future holds nothing for them. Sadness and disappointment led them to separate from the group of disciples and to close in on themselves.

How many men and women, faced with suffering, evil, and death, take the same path and turn in on themselves, break with others, and fall into despair? How many baptized Christians are disappointed in what they expect from the church, from the Christian religion, and have gradually cut themselves off from any contact with the Christian community?

Second attitude: They look for meaning in the events
(vv. 15, 19-24)

But these two travelers are not completely lost. "They were conversing."[15] Thus they do not report the the death of Jesus in a neutral manner. They remain intrigued by what has happened and they are trying to find meaning in it. They say they are "overwhelmed" by the story of the women who report another version of the event: Jesus is "alive" according to the witness of angels. They speak openly with the one who has posed questions to them and who has lent them an attentive ear (vv. 19-24). They are looking for meaning.

The search for meaning—often provoked by painful events—that calls into question the directions we have chosen in life often opens the possibility of discovering a new horizon. The Good News may find a way to be heard.

Third attitude: They let themselves be challenged and enlightened by the one who has listened to them (v. 25)

"Oh, how foolish you are! How slow of heart to believe all that the prophets spoke!" These are strong, disturbing words! What follows shows us that the disciples did not take offense at these challenging words that called them into question. They are open to the words of the one who invited them to speak and who listened to their whole story.

If people do not accept being challenged and having their self-ish vision and the priority of their values called into question, if they remain absorbed in the pursuit of possessions and power, for example, it is impossible to go any further in proclaiming the Gospel of Jesus Christ and the God he reveals. It is not the time for evangelizing with words. The witness of a Christian life might eventually open the way to raising the question.

Fourth attitude: They accept the invitation to stop seeing the Messiah as the answer to their needs and their dreams of glory. They are now open to a vision of life that includes passing by the way of suffering (vv. 26-27)

In the story of Emmaus, it is clear that the two travelers, like Jesus, were familiar with the Scriptures, but they did a selective reading of those documents, choosing passages that fit with their desire for a socio-political kingdom. Jesus broadens their horizon and thus corrects their vision. They allow themselves to be divested of their false images of God and of his action in their life. The rest of the story shows, in effect, that Jesus' teachings produce a transformation. He enlightened these "foolish men." "He interpreted to them what referred to him in all the Scriptures," and he warmed the hearts of these men who were "so slow to believe."[16] "Were not our hearts burning [within us] while he spoke to us on the way and opened the scriptures to us?" (v. 32).

In order to be truly converted and then make progress in the life of faith, we must, at various moments in life, renounce images of God to which we have been attached. God is always beyond our categories, especially the categories defined by our spontaneous needs and desires. Recognition of God and of Jesus Christ in our life can only come at the cost of purification.[17]

Fifth attitude: They express a desire that becomes a prayer (v. 29)

As they begin to take stock of their blindness and allow their hearts to be warmed by the Word, a desire rises up in them, a desire that turns to prayer: "Stay with us." We might use the following words to fill in the reason for their invitation: "We would like to get to know you!" They thirst for his presence, not only for knowledge about him. This thirst is expressed in prayer. They want to know more about Jesus, they want to know more about God!—not as a stranger, but as someone close, as a friend. Now there can be a time of sharing; now the encounter can take place.

The rest will be up to Jesus, who accepts the invitation—responds to the prayer—sits down at table with them and with a gesture opens their eyes to recognize him (vv. 29-30).

The story of Emmaus is interesting on a symbolic level. It begins in the daytime, but the hearts of the disciples are in darkness. It ends at night, when the disciples are enlightened—basking in the sunlight—in the presence of the living Lord Jesus.

Sixth attitude: They recognize him in faith (vv. 31-32)

"With that their eyes were opened and they recognized him, but he vanished from their sight." Recognized with the eyes of faith, Jesus disappears to the eyes of the flesh. He is not absent; now he dwells within the disciples. And a fruit of this interior presence is the fact that they experience a strong sense of communion with each other.

It takes a personal act of faith to recognize Jesus present in the signs that are given to us. It is not a question of evidence that convinces us. The story of Emmaus presents three privileged places of this presence in our lives: the events (vv. 13-24), the Word of Scripture (v. 25-27), and the Eucharist (vv. 28-32). But the act of faith is always a free act of commitment.

Seventh attitude: They get involved with the church and become witnesses (vv. 33-35)

"So they set out at once and returned to Jerusalem."[18] There they rejoin the group of disciples who confirm for them the reality of the resurrection of Jesus, recognized as "Lord," and they in their turn "recounted what had taken place on the way and how he was made known to them in the breaking of the bread." To this entire group of his gathered disciples Jesus manifests himself once again. He officially gives them the mandate to be his witnesses in the world and promises to send the Spirit to help them accomplish their mission (vv. 36-49).

Faith does not come to a halt when we recognize the presence of Jesus Christ in our lives. This encounter draws us into the community of Christians—the church—and pushes us outwards toward others in order to bear witness to him.[19] The mission is only possible in the long run if we belong to the community of disciples and receive its support.

"The Lord has truly been raised and has appeared to Simon!"[20] This proclamation by the gathered group of disciples is the heart of the kerygma. Thus, in following this last model of evangelization, we come back to the first model, the kerygmatic approach presented in the first chapter of this book. This model is the quintessence of the testimony about Jesus spoken by the apostles and disciples in the missionary discourses of the Acts of the Apostles.

In the account of Emmaus we have a spiritual journey that presents seven possible attitudes concerning life, Jesus, and the Gospel: (1) sadness, separation and isolation; (2) the quest for meaning manifested in the expression of their desires and their disappointments; (3) listening to God speak through his

Word who enlightens and challenges them; (4) the "warming of their hearts," that is, the discovery of a meaning to life in the Scriptures; (5) prayer that expresses their desire to know Jesus better, to encounter him; (6) communion in the encounter, a communion that happens in faith and that passes by the sacraments (the Eucharist in our text);[21] and (7) commitment to the mission in order to become, in their turn, for other people, signs and instruments of the encounter with Christ.

It is also possible to translate the transformation that has taken place in them by saying that they passed from sadness ("their faces downcast") to joy ("they set out that instant and returned to Jerusalem"), from isolation to communion, from disengagement to commitment.[22]

The Evangelizer Must Be Evangelized

Each stage of the spiritual journey described by this story could take months, even years. We should also note that this journey is not a linear trajectory that is accomplished once and for all. Often in our Christian and missionary life, we pass through—or revisit—one or another stage of the journey. The spiritual life is marked by crises and moments of deepening. The disciple of Jesus today is represented in the story of Emmaus both by the two travelers and by Jesus. Rereading this account, we are called to meditate on and pray with this text all the while examining where we are on our spiritual journey of "becoming Christian" and becoming a "witness."

We also pass through moments of doubt in faith, moments when we lack hope, moments when we neglect to be nourished by the Bread of the Gospel Word and the Eucharist. We are evangelizers in constant need of being evangelized. We are always on the way, in need of conversion. Where are we at this moment on the route of becoming more human and on the path of progress toward deeper Christian faith? We should ask ourselves: do I neglect the encounter with Jesus Christ in my life, in the Word of God, in the Eucharist? We should reread and meditate on the text personally, following the journey of the two disciples who have left the community with their hopes dashed. We believers should perhaps deconstruct in ourselves this false conviction that everything must always go smoothly for us on the level of our faith. If we ourselves have experienced doubts and resistance in our journey of faith, this may allow us to communicate better with the people we are called to evangelize. Manifesting in our testimony some of this modesty—this fragility—in our belief is reassuring for persons we encounter who experience a lack of certainty or some hesitation about making an act of faith.

In addition, the testimony we need to give is not only for people who are not committed to the Christian life. Christians are called to evangelize each other in an ongoing way, for evangelization is never completed, even with people who are themselves engaged in religious life or ecclesial ministries.

The story of Emmaus can also be read in another way, as a method of continuing evangelization for Christian communities. In this account, Luke is telling people in his community (and therefore us too) that they can constantly come into contact with the risen Jesus:

- He is present in your life. He is walking with you in the midst of your occupations and your preoccupations. Discover him! Open your heart to his Presence!
- He is present in the Sacred Scriptures. Meditate on them, allow your heart to be warmed by contact with them!
- He is present in the Eucharistic bread. Receive in faith this wonderful gift of his Presence!

The Mission: Giving and Receiving

Can we say something else on the relationship between the evangelizer and the evangelized? I once heard Henri Nouwen, an author famous for his spiritual writings, say that evangelization is not only setting out to tell others about the Good News of the risen Lord, but also receiving it from those to whom we have been sent. I would add that God is already present and acting in the lives of the persons we meet, no matter how far they may think they are from God. The other, even if he or she identifies as a nonbeliever, has human experience and perhaps even spiritual experience. From this encounter and sharing, our own human and spiritual life may well be enriched.[23] We are evangelized even by those we evangelize.

I have been personally touched by the witness of a confrere in my missionary community, who spent his whole priestly ministry in Africa and, after returning to France at a very advanced age, continues his mission efforts there. He writes: "More and more I believe that, in our world today, mission is about encounter, about hospitality. It is going to meet the other with what I am and welcoming what he or she is in order to let ourselves be enriched and transformed by one another. My ministerial priesthood is to be found there and that requires a great capacity for listening, a great capacity for openness and a 'contemplative' soul. That is what Jesus the Christ did, and that is what I am called to do."[24]

After reading and contemplating the story of Emmaus, Christian readers may well feel invited to continue their personal reflection with questions like the following. What is my Christian and missionary approach with people in my environment who are far from the church? Is it solidarity? Is it an awakening? Is it enlightening by means of the Word of the Gospel? Is it another approach entirely? What are the questions, the preoccupations, the disappointed hopes of the people who make up the context of my life and mission?

The Two Disciples on the Road to Emmaus: Could It be a Couple?

As we come to the end of our reflections we might be wondering who these two travelers are. Only one is given a name, Cleopas. In the ordinary presentation of the story, the two travelers are identified as two men. A number of great artists, especially at the time of the Renaissance, presented the scene of the meal in the setting of an inn where the two men stopped with Jesus upon their arrival at Emmaus. The NABRE, however, withholds from speculating on the gender of the second traveler. In his recent highly regarded commentary on the Gospel of Luke, François Bovon mentions the hypothesis proposed by some authors, that the two disciples are a couple, a man and his wife. But he discards this possibility without discussing it.[25]

Three reasons lead me to lean toward this hypothesis of a couple, a man and his wife:[26] First of all, in Luke's gospel, the group of disciples that accompanied Jesus during his public ministry included men and women. In Luke 8:1-3 we read: "Afterward he journeyed from one town and village to another, preaching and proclaiming the Good News of the kingdom of God. Accompanying him were the Twelve and some women." Among them Mary Magdalene is mentioned.[27] We find these women once again at the cross: "all his acquaintances stood at a distance, including the women who had followed him from Galilee and saw these events" (Luke 23:49). "The women who had come from Galilee with him followed behind, and when they had seen the tomb and the way in which his body was laid in it, they returned and prepared spices and perfumed oils" (Luke 23:55). In chapter 24, the two episodes that surround the story of the disciples at Emmaus mention several of these women disciples who have come to the tomb, find it empty, have a vision of angels, and report their experience "to the eleven and the others." In the story of Emmaus, Cleopas will speak of them as being "some women from our group." No doubt they were among the group of the "eleven and their companions" that the two disciples of Emmaus will find at Jerusalem and to whom Jesus will appear and entrust the mission of being his witnesses (Luke 24:1-9, 22, 33, 36, 48).

In addition, only one of the two disciples is named in the account of Emmaus, Cleopas (Luke 24:18). But the name of the other disciple most likely appears in an important gospel passage. Indeed, John the evangelist mentions that at the foot of the cross of Jesus "stood his mother, and his mother's sister, Mary the wife of Clopas, and Mary of Magdala" (John 19:25). On the road to Emmaus, Cleopas is the only disciple whose name appears. At that time it would be normal, if a traveling couple met someone on the road, that the first member of the couple to speak would be the husband. In ancient Greek documents the names we find in the gospels ("Clopas" in John and "Cleopas" in Luke) are frequently interchanged.

Finally, the account of the disciples at Emmaus says: "As they approached the village to which they were going, he gave the impression that he was going on farther, but they urged him, 'Stay with us'" (Luke 24:28-29). Some recent scholars have noted that this is consistent with the customs of Palestinian hospitality at the time, such that the travelers likely arrived at their own home. It is precisely because previous commentators presupposed that these two persons were men that most exegetes imagined they were arriving at an inn, since it was unthinkable at the time that two men would share the same dwelling. The more natural reading of verse 24 is, then: The two disciples, Cleopas and his wife Mary, arrived at their home in Emmaus at nightfall, and they pressed Jesus to stay with them.

Conclusion

The route we have followed in the present volume presupposes that the Bible is our first reference not only for the content of evangelization but for the methods or approaches to take in communicating the Good News. The Bible, the Word of God in human language, is constructed from stories and discourses. Knowing how Jesus and the apostles went about their task of evangelizing is a reference and model for our mission as disciples called to bear witness today. The presentation offered here does not pretend to cover all the biblical models of evangelization, but those chosen and described are especially significant.

They have in common the following point. Evangelizers start with people, with their human and spiritual quest such as they present it, and with their language. But at the same time, evangelizers add something new by their way of being and eventually by their words: they pose questions and open the way to an encounter with the Lord. Thus the option for Jesus Christ and the God he bears witness to is not imposed as a proof; it remains a challenge, a "risk" to take that is left to personal freedom. We will elaborate a little on this point.

In the kerygmatic model, the apostles addressing the Jews start with their shared acceptance of the First Covenant and the longing for the Messiah. They begin with the well-known fact of the life and death of Jesus. Essentially they argue from the Scriptures that are accepted by the people to affirm a fact that is not verifiable by the people—the Resurrection of Jesus and his existence as Christ and Lord. Working from this fact, they correct the common vision of the expected messiah as a long-awaited political savior.

In the model of Athens, Paul begins with the Athenians' knowledge of God and their religious quest. In the Greek universe where the First Testament is not a reference point and where there is no expectation of a messiah, he opens the horizon on a revelation of the "unknown God" they long to know, whose existence is revealed by a man God has raised from the dead.

In the evangelical model, Jesus bears witness by his person and his life to a new image of God and of the Messiah of God, which is rooted in the revelation of the First Testament but which also goes beyond it. Jesus is the "incarnate" face, the human face of God. Jesus, a man of compassion, by his life and by his words indicates the way to human happiness. Today, this humanist vision of God's messenger responds well to the kind of quest we often come across in our secularized world.

In the model of Emmaus, the risen Jesus starts with the disciples' desire and expectation of the Messiah. But he has to help them recognize that they have not understood his message and his person during their journey with him before his death. A model for bearing witness is in interpersonal relations where the part played by the mind, the part played by the heart, the part played by listening, and the part played by the word come together in harmony in such a way that the process of evangelization remains profoundly and entirely human.

The four biblical models of evangelization presented here can well serve as inspiration for the evangelizer today, each one corresponding to a different life situation of the people to whom we want to communicate the Good News. One might think that in the testimony they render to people, today's Christian evangelizers will be called to use these models not in the order in which they were presented here but in reverse order. First, listen to people, let them speak of their suffering, their disappointments, their questions, and so forth (the model of Emmaus). Then bear witness by one's life and eventually by words of the compassion and of the happy ("blessed") life that Jesus lived and that he offered his disciples (the model of evangelical humanism). Then cultivate openness to the transcendent, to the eternal God (the model of Athens). And finally proclaim one's own faith in Jesus as Christ and Lord (the kerygmatic model). In practice, these various forms of witness may well overlap. Being attentive to the experience of each person to whom we proclaim the Living Lord Jesus Christ, we will find that different but complementary methods have their place in the mission of the church.

In fact, these models are not mutually exclusive—quite the contrary! In bearing witness, Christians can use the various models in a complementary way. In the end, we might well say that these approaches need each other. For example, how can evangelizers witness to the risen Jesus as the source of hope (the kerygmatic model) if, in their personal lives, they do not draw inspiration from the humanism of compassion (evangelical model) and if they do not listen carefully and take into consideration the experience of the person before whom they are called to bear witness (the Emmaus model)?

Studying these models invites us to stay within the framework of our world and culture—largely secularized in the West—and to enter into the human journey of people where they are and, by our ways of being and acting, and at an opportune moment, by words, to be a sign. People's points of access to the Gospel are many and varied. Some will be ready to hear us talk explicitly about Jesus Christ, about the love and the liberation he brings us. Others will be searching for an absolute in their lives and will thirst for God. And a third group will simply need a compassionate presence, someone to listen or to offer generous help in a difficult situation.

Evangelization has to be adapted to every country, to every cultural milieu, and to every person. There is no single recipe for evangelization! But it does include fundamental components and a single objective that the present work is intended to present.

It is also important to be conscious that the God of Jesus Christ remains mysterious and the ways of meeting him are often unpredictable. The disciples of Jesus Christ need to present God as a mystery to be discovered, a mystery always beyond our grasp, but always part of our reality. Perhaps today people can more easily accept the mystery of God because we have a better sense of the mystery of our world and we are more aware that we cannot know or control it completely.

The method of learning about God and about what he has to offer, as it is presented in the New Testament, should be our guide. On the one hand it implies shaking up, calling into question people's narrow desires (Luke 24:21, 25). On the other hand, it involves starting with the positive, with the best of what they are already experiencing. We have to come into contact with the image of God inscribed in the depths of persons, that is, we have to build on the strengths and the dynamic forces that are in them rather than on their weaknesses, we have to start with experiences that can foster the greatest kind of dreams. At a certain moment, we have to speak about the Gospel message in order to call forth their desire to open themselves to what Jesus Christ has to offer. "But how can they call on him in whom they have not believed? And how can they believe in him of whom they have not heard, and how can they hear without someone to preach?" (Rom 10:14). The word of the Gospel can warm hearts and give a taste for God (Luke 24:32). But then we are in a second stage of evangelizing witness.[1]

Upon finishing their reading about the biblical models presented in this work, Christian readers can take some time to stop and meditate on the following questions. What is the biblical model that touched me personally, that corresponds to my personality, to my formation, to my way of being Christian? Which of these biblical approaches seems to respond best to the situation of the people to whom I am called to proclaim the Gospel message?

The Evangelizer in "Search" of God

Reflecting on the new evangelization, we Christians should look at our own needs in order to understand better the needs of those around us. Speaking to American bishops on November 26, 2011, Benedict XVI said: "Evangelization appears not simply as a task to be undertaken *ad extra*; we ourselves are the first to need re-evangelization." We could also say that disciples of Jesus Christ, called to bear witness to their faith, should themselves be committed to a personal process of ongoing evangelization. The four models presented here are also to be taken in complementary fashion for our own progress in the personal life of faith. We have to live them and to integrate them in the course of our life. We are not Christians all at once or once and for all; we become Christians gradually. Have I really made a choice for Jesus as my Lord and my Savior? Have I encountered God? Does he remain present in my life, at the deepest level of my being? Am I becoming more "human" with the passage of the years—more attentive to others, to their suffering and their needs, more compassionate? How do I behave in my encounters with those who have not encountered Jesus Christ?

In our secularized world, many people are looking for the way to become fully human. They are "seekers." We Catholics can project an image that says we are no long "seekers" because we are "installed" in our church: we "possess God." Mission in secularity implies dialogue. We will be able to dialogue with the people around us to the extent that we are "searching" for God. God is always beyond the way we represent him. He is always mysterious. We need to be seekers of God, seekers of Christ, as St. Paul writes in the letter to his dear Philippians: "I continue my pursuit toward the goal, the prize of God's upward calling, in Christ Jesus" (Phil 3:12).

Evangelization in Christian Communities

We have to add an important clarification at this point. What we have been saying throughout this book about the disciple who is called to be an evangelizer should also be said of the church as a Christian community and as an institution in all its dimensions. How can the testimony of an individual disciple bear fruit if it is contradicted by the image that the church projects as an institution? Is it not the entire church, as the community of believers and as institution, that is called to follow Jesus and his apostles, in its manner of being, in its manner of working (in its structures), and of bearing witness? More precisely, it should be centered on Jesus Christ and the Gospel, bearing witness to a God of Love, living the Beatitudes and the compassion that so marked the life of Jesus, and listening to the experience of societies and persons, all the while drawing inspiration from Jesus on the road to Emmaus. May this be its ideal, even if, as it consists of individual persons, it remains fragile and fallible.

Reflection on the mission of evangelization entrusted to the members of the church should be completed with a reflection on the quality of life of Christian communities. On this subject, the book of the Acts of the Apostles is a fundamental reference. We could meditate, in particular, on the three brief summaries at the beginning of the Acts that present the life of the first Christian communities and the power of their witness (Acts 2:42-47).[2] The "fraternal communion" (*koinōnia* in Greek) that marked these communities was powerfully attractive: there was unity among the Christians, rooted in the union of each person with Christ and leading to a sharing on a material and a spiritual level, according to the needs of each member of the community. In his letters St. Paul describes in a similar way the *koinōnia* that he considered essential in every Christian community. Note that among the first Christians themselves, *koinōnia* was lived imperfectly, a fact made clear especially in the conflicts reported in the Acts of the Apostles. It is clear that reflection is necessary in order to discern how *koinōnia* is called to take form in our societies today.

A question arises: when nonbelievers or nonpracticing Catholics come into Catholic churches, for example, for baptisms, marriages, or funerals, what kind of testimony of a happy and hopeful life do our communities give? The most profound expression of a link between community and mission is found in the Gospel of John. "This is how all will know that you are my disciples, if you have love for one another" (John 13:35; see also 17:11, 21-23). Do people see that the members of a Christian community help each other or, more simply, that they are happy together?

A crucial element of the process of evangelization is the way new adult converts are received into Christian communities. These new converts, full of fervor, hope to find members who are living the Gospel in their new community. Do we not need to establish, on the parish level as well as the diocesan level, in addition to agents for the various dimensions of pastoral ministry, a ministry for the coordination of evangelization that can look after, among other things, welcoming and integrating the new converts into the life of the church?[3]

"The Holy Spirit and Ourselves . . ."

Peter, Paul, and the other participants in the Assembly of Jerusalem, which we can consider the first council in the church, introduced the decisions taken by that assembly with this formula; thus they resolved the first great conflict in the church (Acts 15:28). Although it is done much more modestly, it is always with this formula that the disciples of Jesus Christ accept and live out their mission to proclaim him in their own milieu. We cannot end our reflections on evangelization without recalling this essential point that the power of being witnesses comes from the Holy Spirit in us: ". . . you will receive power when the Holy Spirit comes upon you, and you will be my witnesses" (Acts 1:8; see also 1 Cor 12:3). The Spirit is received in prayer (Acts 1:14; 2:1; 4:31). The Spirit gives the capacity to bear witness with "boldness," that is, with freedom and courage (this is the sense of the Greek word *parrèsia*, which is repeated twelve times in the Acts of the Apostles from 2:29 to 28:31).

The witness is not alone nor left to his or her own devices in bearing witness. The work of evangelization is first of all the work of the Holy Spirit, who inspires and supports the disciples of Jesus Christ in announcing the Good News, and who is also active within the persons to whom the disciples are called to proclaim it. The fruitfulness of this action of the Spirit within the persons who receive the message remains incalculable today, just as it was in apostolic times.

Regardless of the approach we take in evangelizing or the testimony we give about Jesus Christ and the God of Jesus Christ, faith will never be the result of rational proof. We can never demonstrate by rational arguments the reality of the risen Jesus Christ and of the God he has revealed to us. The act of faith always remains a free act of the will that, however, must also be rational. And it is the duty of the disciples of Jesus Christ who are called to bear witness to their Christian faith, to contribute by their testimony to making it not only reasonable but desirable.

The Taste for Jesus Christ and for the Gospel

We end this work on the ways of evangelizing today by underlining a fundamental objective of evangelization. To evangelize is first of all awakening a desire: the longing for the Gospel, the longing for Jesus Christ, the longing for the God of Jesus Christ.[4] The Gospel should truly be perceived for what it means etymologically: Good News. The Gospel is essentially a message of love, and human beings are made for love, because they are created in the image of God. We must distance ourselves from the Protestant vision of the sixteenth century, which holds the total corruption of human nature and which took the form of Jansenism in the Catholic Church. The human being is fundamentally good! In the four models contemplated in the present work, the Gospel, whether presented by Jesus, by Peter, or by Paul, awakens persons to the best in themselves and appeals to their best and deepest desires or awakens these desires.

The mission of evangelization is a matter of inviting people to rediscover their profound longing, despite their apparent desires: the desire for possessions, for power, and for pleasure. Satisfying one's needs is legitimate. But to achieve personal fulfillment, to really succeed in life, to be truly happy, we have to rediscover our profound longing to love and to be loved, to find it once again and try to respond to it. Need is functional; it is something that drives us inwards. Desire is relational; it turns us toward others and ultimately toward God, for human beings are made for communion. Surely that is the message we can draw from the story of Jesus with the two travelers on the road to Emmaus. They revealed the hopes they had put in a political liberator who might satisfy their needs. After listening to them, Jesus challenges them and, with the light of the Scriptures, he opens the horizon of their desires. Isn't that what evangelization is all about: starting with what people are experiencing and then gently opening their minds to something more, something better?

Whatever approach we take to bear witness to the Christian faith and render it not only acceptable but desirable, the act of faith will always be an event of grace: at one and the same time, it is a decision taken in human freedom and a gift of God.

Notes

Introduction (pages 1–4)

1. "We wish to confirm once more that the task of evangelizing all people constitutes the essential mission of the Church" (*Evangelii Nuntiandi* 14); "*The Church is missionary by her very nature*, for Christ's mandate is not something contingent or external, but reaches the very heart of the Church." (*Redemptoris Missio* 62).

2. Benedict XVI, *Verbum Domini* (Post-Synodal Apostolic Exhortation on the Word of God), September 30, 2010.

3. Marcel Dumais, *Le langage de l'évangélisation* (Montreal: Bellarmin, 1976), 400.

4. I would mention in particular: Marcel Dumais, *Communauté et mission. Une lecture des Actes des Apôtres pour aujourd'hui*, Relais-Études 10 (Paris: Desclée, 1992); later revised and enlarged as *Communauté et mission. Une relecture des Actes des Apôtres* (Montreal: Bellarmin, 2000).

Chapter 1 (pages 5–18)

1. In the *motu proprio* he appointed Archbishop Rino Fisichella president of the new Council.

2. Pope Benedict XVI, introduction to *Ubicumque et semper*, September 21, 2010.

3. In effect, we can understand the expression "new evangelization" to mean a renewal of evangelization, or more simply, a question of giving a high priority to evangelization.

4. Pope Benedict launched this appeal once again in his apostolic exhortation *Verbum Domini* (2010): "a great many Christians . . . need to have the word of God once more persuasively proclaimed to them, so that they can concretely experience the power of the Gospel" (96).

5. It has been pointed out, however, that the expression "new evangelization" was used in a document published by the bishops of Latin America at the time of their conference in Medellin in 1968.

6. John Paul II was also to speak of new evangelization of the "first world," which, in certain contexts, includes not only the countries of Europe but also countries like Canada and the United States.

7. Pope Benedict XVI, *Africae Munus* (Apostolic Exhortation on the Church in Africa), November 19, 2011, 159–71. The quote is taken from no. 171.

8. If fewer and fewer people living in the Western world choose to believe in Jesus Christ and in the God of Jesus Christ, then reference to the Gospel, and consequently so-called "Christian values," will lose their social influence in the West.

9. For example, when Benedict XVI first announced the forthcoming creation of a Pontifical Council for the Promotion of the New Evangelization, he described its objective in the following terms: "to promote a renewed evangelization in the countries where the first proclamation of the faith has already resonated and where Churches with an ancient foundation exist but are experiencing the progressive secularization of society and a sort of 'eclipse of the sense of God'" (Homily on the Solemnity of Saints Peter and Paul, Basilica of Saint Paul Outside the Walls, June 28, 2010).

10. One may speak of secular society, but also of secular culture. One would say that the reality of secularization in many countries of the West is such that the culture no longer conveys in itself the transcendent. It no longer transmits the sense of God. What was formerly a "Christian" culture is no longer Christian.

11. *Le Monde des Religions* 21 (January 2007).

12. A majority (79 percent) identify God as a "force, energy or spirit." Nonetheless, 58 percent of those who say they are "Catholic" believe in the resurrection of Christ and 74 percent think that death is not the last stage of human existence (of these, 10 percent uphold the resurrection of the dead and 8 percent believe in reincarnation on earth in another life). French Catholics, for the most part (76 percent) have a positive view of the church and of Pope Benedict (71 percent).

13. "La France deviant-elle athée?" (Is France Becoming Atheist?), *Le Monde des Religions* 49 (September/October 2011): 18–19.

14. This study does have a limitation. It was conducted with a sample of 1,000 individuals, but it was done through the Internet, thus excluding people who do not use this technology.

15. Charles Taylor, *A Secular Age* (Cambridge, MA: Harvard University Press, 2007).

16. Ibid., 3.

17. *Le Monde des Religions* 49 (September/October 2011), 18–19.

18. *Présence Magazine* (November 2011), 5.

19. Cardinal Dolan, "The Announcement of the Gospel Today: Between *missio ad gentes* and the New Evangelization," Address to the College of Cardinals, February 17, 2012.

20. There is a significant difference in culture with regard to religion between the United States and Canada. In the United States, public invocation of God by the president and members of governing bodies ("God bless America!") and public statements about belonging to a Christian church are normal and are considered helpful politically. In Canada, such public expressions by those in political leadership are considered politically counterproductive. In Canada, it is important to consider separately the situation of the aboriginal peoples and immigrants whose cultures include a relationship to the transcendent.

21. Joseph Ratzinger, *Salt of the Earth: Christianity and the Catholic Church at the End of the Millennium* (San Francisco: Ignatius, 1997), 255–56.

22. Ibid., 265.

23. Ibid., 268–69.

24. Ibid., 272.

25. The disciples to whom Jesus appeared include some women and the two disciples on the road to Emmaus, who returned to the community of disciples after having left with their hopes dashed. We will come back to this in chapter 6.

26. Acts 2:29; 4:13, 29, 31; 9:27, 28; 13:46; 14:3; 18:26; 19:8; 26:26; 28:31. In all these verses the Greek term (*parrèsia*) is used. It indicates both courage and boldness in the witnessing.

27. The document that was produced by the fifth meeting of CELAM at Aparecida (Brazil) in May 2007 developed this point very well. But Paul VI had clearly affirmed the point in *Evangelii Nuntiandi* in 1975: "Finally, the person who has been evangelized goes on to evangelize others. Here lies the test of truth, the touchstone of evangelization: it is unthinkable that a person should accept the Word and give himself to the kingdom without becoming a person who bears witness to it and proclaims it in his turn" (24).

28. Pope Benedict XVI, *Porta fidei* (Motu Proprio on Faith), October 11, 2011.

29. Here the pope is citing his own encyclical, *Deus caritas est* (Encyclical Letter on Christian Love), December 25, 2005, 1.

30. The citations in this paragraph are taken from *Porta fidei* 7 and from Pope Benedict's discourse on October 15, 2011, during a Congress on the New Evangelization with the promulgation of *Porta fidei*. The date of the opening of the Year of Faith was intended to mark the twentieth anniversary of the publication of *The Catechism of the Catholic Church*. The pope also invites the faithful to come to a systematic knowledge of the contents of the faith expressed in this catechism (*Porta fidei*, 11–12).

31. For example, he writes to the Christian community at Corinth that he had evangelized: "Since, then, we have the same spirit of faith, according to which it is written, 'I believed, therefore I spoke,' we too believe and therefore speak" (2 Cor 4:13).

32. One could expand this study to cover God's teaching methods throughout the entirety of biblical revelation. I think that, in general, individuals baptized as infants often unconsciously follow the same paths of discovering God that the chosen people trod. They pass through the "God of the Old Testament" before arriving, sometimes after a long journey of faith, at the "God of Jesus" (the God of Love).

Chapter 2 (pages 19–36)

1. Acts 2:22-39; 3:12-26; 4:9-12; 5:29-32; 10:34-43; 13:16-41.

2. In the other missionary discourses of the Acts of the Apostles, other titles are given to Jesus: Prince of Life (3:15; 5:31), Savior (5:31; 13:23), Judge of the living and the dead (10:42). These are aspects of these two fundamental dimensions, Lord and Christ.

3. A person cannot be called a Christian without adhering to the kerygma. To believe in Jesus Lord and Christ is to believe that salvation is in him.

4. See also 1 Cor 12:3; 2 Cor 1:2; Phil 2:11.

5. The most beautiful catechisms do not convert. But, obviously, they can nourish the faith of one who is already converted.

6. In his gospel, Luke underlines the central theme of Jesus' preaching: "To the other towns also I must proclaim the good news of the kingdom of God, because for this purpose I have been sent" (Luke 4:43). In the Acts of the Apostles, Luke shows that in proclaiming the kerygma the apostles teach that with the resurrection of Jesus the kingdom of God has begun in our world (Acts 8:12; 14:22; 19:8; 20:25; 28:23, 31).

7. He repeats this message twice: "But now Christ has been raised from the dead, the firstfruits of those who have fallen asleep" (1 Cor 15:20, 23). And again two more times: "If there is no resurrection of the dead, Christ himself cannot have been raised" (1 Cor 15:13); and "For if the dead are not raised, neither has Christ been raised" (1 Cor 15:16).

8. Charles Péguy, *The Portal of the Mystery of Hope*, trans. David Louis Schindler, Jr., Ressourcement: Retrieval and Renewal in Catholic Thought (Grand Rapids, MI: Wm B. Eerdmans, 1996).

9. "Being Christian is born not of an ethical decision or a lofty ideal, but an encounter with an event, a person, which gives life a new horizon and a decisive direction" (Benedict XVI, *Africae Munus* 165). Once again the pope takes up here a phrase he used in the introduction to his first encyclical, *Deus*

Caritas Est, published six years earlier. It appeared as the fundamental inspiration of the pontificate of Benedict XVI. He often referred to it. At the end of our first chapter, we cited the last part of this phrase, used by the pope in October 2011 when he announced the Year of Faith: "The Year of Faith, from this perspective, is a summons to an authentic and renewed conversion to the Lord, the one Savior of the world" (*Porta Fidei* 6).

10. Kerygma is to catechesis what birth is to growth: it precedes it, and it is even the condition for the possibility of a truly fruitful catechesis. I cite at this point a sentence from the report of the European Congress for catechesis that took place in May of 2012: "Catechesis is not just indoctrination but it is above all experience of God."

11. There are three stages of mission in the church since the time of its foundation: 1) first, there is the kerygma (the initial evangelization); 2) then the catechesis of the converts, which gave birth to the gospels; 3) then the sacraments. The sacraments of Christian initiation, baptism and the Eucharist, have been practiced since the formation of the first Christian communities.

12. See page 120, note 11.

13. Ideally, all preaching should be rooted in the kerygma and lead to it!

14. Life on earth was perceived and often even presented in preaching as "a valley of tears." Life after death was going to reverse this situation.

15. In the United States, the Southern Baptist minister Billy Graham was one of the first to make this kerygmatic presentation of the Good News in large assemblies and in the media. His approach is more balanced than many of the "televangelists" who followed him.

16. Vincent J. Donovan, *Christianity Rediscovered* (Maryknoll, NY: Orbis, 2003).

17. Marcel Dumais, *Le langage de l'évangélisation. L'annonce missionaire en milieu juif (Actes 13:16-41)* (Montreal: Bellarmin, 1974).

18. This is also the case in Peter's discourse on Pentecost, which we examined at the beginning of this chapter.

19. The Greek noun *epaggelia* (promise) is found in the two "hinge" verses in the discourse of Paul in vv. 23 and 32.

20. *Anistēmi* in 2 Sam 7:12, in the Septuagint (Greek Old Testament), is the same verb *anistēmi* in Acts 13:33-34.

21. Jean Ladriere, *L'Articulation du sens* (Paris: DDB, 1970), 227–41. Paul Ricoeur has passages in several of his works on symbol. In particular one could read several passages in *Le conflit des interprétations* (Paris: Seuil, 1969), 15–23, 32, 64–79, 283–86, 313–18.

22. But we must add that, in determining the meaning, the Jesus event has a unique reach: it is presented, in effect, as the decisive event in history—the eschatological event—not only for the Jewish people but for all humanity.

23. Remember the simple fact that Peter and Paul were preaching to people—the Jews—who believed in God and were waiting for the Savior Messiah.

24. "The Good News proclaimed by the witness of life sooner or later has to be proclaimed by the word of life" (*Evangelii Nuntiandi* 22).

25. Acts 2:42-7; 4:32-5; 5:13-14.

Chapter 3 (pages 37–57)

1. Note the attention Paul gives to the particular situation of this peasant people of Lystra. Leaning on the beliefs of the day, he points out that the living God he is speaking about is the God of rain and of fertility. The Creator God "gave you rains from heaven and fruitful seasons, and filled you with nourishment and gladness for your hearts" (v. 17).

2. Behind this interpretation, it is possible to see the influence of a certain Lutheran exegesis, where the letters of Paul serve as "a canon within the canon" and where the option of faith is not accompanied by a philosophical line of thought or use of reason.

3. A.-J. Festugière, "Saint Paul à Athènes et la Première Épître aux Corinthiens," *La Vie Intellectuelle*, no. 34 (1935): 357–69.

4. A neuralgic point in the debate is the interpretation given to the declaration of the hearers at the end of Paul's discourse: "we would like to hear you on this some other time." Some exegetes (for example, Haenchen, Roloff, Schneider) interpret this sentence as a polite but firm rejection of the message of Paul; others (Barrett, Johnson, Marshall, Polhill, Fitzmyer), on the contrary, see here a real interest in Paul's message. In his work *Nouvelles Études sur les Actes des Apôtres*, the great French-speaking specialist on the Acts of the Apostles, Jacques Dupont, supports the latter position, which is my own (he cites my study on the discourse at Athens, "Le langage évangélique et la vie en cours: Réflexions sur le modèle biblique," *Église et Théologie* 7 (1976): 147–70.

5. Luke, in the Acts of the Apostles, presents models of missionary preaching. These are not recipes that guarantee success.

6. The discourse at Athens has two parts; the second (17:30-31) corresponds to the first (17:23-29). In fact, verses 23 and 30 use the same terms: "To an *Unknown* God. What therefore you unknowingly worship, I proclaim to you" (v. 23); "God has overlooked the times of ignorance, but now he demands that all people everywhere repent" (v. 30).

7. Before presenting Paul's discourse at Athens, the author of the Acts of the Apostles notes that "even some of the Epicurean and Stoic philosophers engaged him in discussion" (Acts 17:18).

8. Compare the Greek version of the Septuagint with the Hebrew text in the following passages: Gen 2:1; Deut 4:19; 17:3; Is 24:21; 40:26.

9. For example, Zeno, the founder of the Stoic school of philosophy, says: "There is no need to make temples or statues."

10. "God is near you; he is with you; he is within you" (Seneca, *Letters to Lucillus* 41).

11. However, according to the studies done to this point, it does not seem that any ancient Greek text expresses this idea in as clear a manner as Paul does in this speech.

12. At the time of redaction of the New Testament, Stoicism was much more than a philosophical system: it had taken on certain traits of an organized religion, according to Claire Préaux, *Le Monde hellénistique* 2 (Paris: Presses Universitaires de France, 1978), 644–6.

13. Great philosophers who have reflected on "the communication of meaning"—for example, Martin Heidegger in *Being and Time* and Hans Georg Gadamer in *Truth and Method*—say that comprehension starts with a pre-comprehension: it is within the presuppositions of the culture of the hearers that the new meaning is communicated: comprehension comes in its turn to deepen, enrich, or modify and correct the pre-comprehension that has made comprehension possible and that determines it.

14. Before presenting the discourse at the Areopagus, the book of the Acts of the Apostles says that Paul at Athens "was preaching about 'Jesus' and 'Resurrection'" (Acts 17:18). But the primarily theocentric approach Paul takes is understandable after we read in verse 16: "he grew exasperated at the sight of the city full of idols."

15. The discourse at Athens cannot be isolated from its context in Luke–Acts. The image of God with whom everyone is called to enter into communion is revealed in an incomplete way in the discourse of Lystra and Athens. We have to take into account the entire third gospel in order to obtain Luke's portrait of the living God whom Jesus reveals in his fullness.

16. The term "inculturation" has entered into official church documents. The Synod of 1977 used it in its *Message to the People of God*. John Paul II employed it for the first time in an address given to the members of the Pontifical Biblical Commission in 1979.

17. In fact, every human being is called to hear the Word, each one in his or her own language (Acts 2:6–7; 11). The universality of the church is realized gradually, to the extent that each person, each ethnic group, hears the Gospel in its own tongue, that is, incarnated in its culture, whose language is its expression. At Pentecost, people received the Spirit in order to "hear" the Gospel, as the apostles received the Spirit in order to "proclaim" it (Acts 2:4, 11).

18. The discourse at Athens can be considered from other points of view than those developed in the present volume. We can consider it a model of inculturation of the Gospel and an opening to what we would now call inter-religious dialogue.

19. Marcel Dumais, "Le salut en dehors de la foi en Jésus Christ? Observations sur trois passages des Actes des Apôtres," *Église et Théologie* 28 (1997): 161–90.

20. The language of formulations of the faith coming from the Tradition and learned in catechism has its place in the formation of the believer, but that comes at a second moment, in catechesis and in the life of the sacraments, as we have seen in the previous chapter.

21. According to the 2007 *Le Monde des Religions* survey, 79 percent of those who declare themselves as "Catholic" identify God with a "force, energy or spirit." The influence of New Age trends of thought is significant even among Catholics. See above p. 120, n. 11.

22. Augustine, *Confessions* 3.6.11.

23. We can note, for example, the great popularity in French-speaking Canada and in several countries in Europe of books and conferences by the priest-psychologist Jean Monbourquette and his coworker, Isabelle D'Aspremont. They speak about self-esteem and esteem for the Self, the Self being defined as "the spiritual dimension of the person, the soul where the divine dwells."

24. "*Deus intimior intimo meo,*" in the words of St. Augustine: "God closer to me than I am to myself." See n. 22 above.

25. In Quebec, "surveys show that seven young people out of ten say they pray, although the majority say that they do not go to church." Assembly of the Bishops of Quebec, *Proposer aujourd'hui la foi aux jeunes.* (Montreal: Fides, 2000), 28.

26. The famous writer Jean d'Ormesson of the French Academy, who calls himself "an agnostic tempted to believe," admitted in an interview for *Le Monde des Religions* 21 (January/February 2007, 81): "I have a thirst for God . . . a mad desire for God. The figure of Christ fascinates me. The Incarnation is God becoming man; he has to do that to make himself known, and by way of reciprocity, if he becomes man, man becomes God! That is where the power and the beauty of the Christian religion reside."

27. Benedict XVI, address to the Roman Curia, December 21, 2009.

28. For a more developed presentation of the biblical journey that leads to knowledge of the God of Love, see Marcel Dumais, *À la rencontre d'un Dieu-Amour* (Montreal: Médiaspaul, 1999), 128.

Chapter 4 (pages 58–78)

1. Another Christian, the Canadian Jean Vanier, who founded the L'Arche communities in France for handicapped persons, is likewise high on the list of people revered by the general population in France. His communities now exist in many countries. [Translator's note, Father Pierre (who died in 2007

at the age of 95) and Sister Emmanuelle (who died in 2008 just a few days before her hundredth birthday) were much beloved because of their strong support of humanitarian causes.]

2. John Paul II, *Redemptoris Missio* 16.

3. It is after the resurrection of Jesus, after having reflected on the unique quality of the life and person of Jesus, that we arrive at this definition of God. "God is love," the apostle John proclaims twice in his first letter (1 John 4:8, 16). This definition is the fruit of a long reflection, under the guidance of the Holy Spirit, on the fact that Jesus went to the end of love in giving his life for humans (see John 15:13).

4. The Gospel of John, on the other hand, presents a Christology called "descending" (from God to human beings): the Word became flesh (John 1). The Christology of the synoptic gospels is called "ascending": we gradually discover the presence of God, the person of God, in the man Jesus. Nonetheless, the Gospel of John presents admirable examples of the love of Jesus for all human beings, in particular those who are marginal or socially rejected (see his encounter with the Samaritan woman at the well in John 4:1-42; the healing of the paralytic in John 5:1-18; the liberation of the woman caught in adultery in John 8:1-11; the healing of the man born blind in John 9; the washing of the feet in John 13:1-15).

5. "He appointed twelve that they might be with him and he might send them forth to preach" (Mark 3:14). The mission makes sense if it is preceded by "being with him."

6. Mark 8:27, 30; Matt 16:13-20; Luke 9:18-21.

7. In response to the envoys of John the Baptist, who ask if he "is the one who is to come," that is, the Messiah, Jesus replies by applying to himself this same text of Isaiah that he had read in the synagogue (Luke 7:22).

8. On evangelization as including a project of integral human liberation on earth, see Paul VI, *Evangelii Nuntiandi* 30–31; (although this should not "reduce [the] mission [of the church] to the dimensions of a simply temporal project" [32]).

9. Gospel values have played a decisive role in the evolution of human rights in Western societies: e.g., the declarations of human rights associated with the American and French revolutions. See F. Lenoir, *Le Christ philosophe* (Paris: Plon, 2007), 306.

10. The social dimension of the kingdom of God presented by Jesus is not found only in Luke the evangelist, although he does give it special emphasis in his gospel. Think, for example of the famous discourse of Jesus on the last judgment in the Gospel of Matthew: "Come, you who are blessed by my Father. Inherit the kingdom prepared for you from the foundation of the world. For I was hungry and you gave me food, I was thirsty and you gave me drink, a

stranger and you welcomed me, naked and you clothed me, ill and you cared for me, in prison and you visited me. . . whatever you did for one of these least brothers of mine, you did for me" (Matt 25:34-40).

11. In the rest of the New Testament, this verb is found only in four passages of the Gospel of Matthew and four passages in the Gospel of Mark.

12. The NABRE translates it as "moved with/filled with" "pity" or "compassion" in the three stories in Luke's gospel. For readers in certain environments, this translation does not express the richness of the Greek verb.

13. The title provided in the NABRE, "Raising of the Widow's Son," directs the reader of the text, on the other hand, to the account of a miracle (a work manifesting the power of Jesus).

14. He takes care of the man in distress and he makes sure that others will take care of him after his own departure (v. 35).

15. The center of the universe is not me but the other, the unfortunate one. Seeing with the eyes of the heart takes an apprenticeship, which is never at an end.

16. The disciple of Jesus will feel invited to meditate on this parable in another way as well. The Samaritan is Jesus. I am the wounded person who needs a Samaritan. It is the vulnerable or wounded part of me that is in need of healing, compassion, and forgiveness.

17. I have presented a detailed analysis of the parable in two works: Marcel Dumais, "Approche historico-critique d'un texte: la parable du père et de ses deux fils," *L'actualisation du Nouveau Testament* (Paris: Cerf, 1981), 63-95; and *À la rencontre d'un Dieu-Amour* (Montreal: Médiaspaul, 1999), 35-46.

18. In a passage found only in Luke and preceding this magnificent chapter of the gospel, Jesus asks his disciples to imitate him: "When you hold a lunch or a dinner . . . invite the poor, the crippled, the lame, the blind" (Luke 14:12-14). After reading chapter 15, we can understand that this invitation is intended not only—and not even first of all—to relieve the hunger of these poor people. It is a matter of making them come to life, by sharing a meal and the communion it expresses. It is an experience of acknowledging their value as persons and thus of human and spiritual liberation that opens the way to an encounter with the God of compassion.

19. In particular, we could point out that at the heart of this intense human witness of Jesus, we are led to see a transcendent dimension, the relation with one who is beyond humanity, the relation with one whom Jesus calls "Father."

20. *Lineamenta* to the Synod of Bishops, Special Assembly for Asia (1996), 24.

21. *Integral Humanism*: This was the title that the great Christian philosopher Jacques Maritain gave to the work he published in 1936, which became a classic.

22. I have always been impressed by an affirmation often repeated to married couples in the "Marriage Encounter" movement, which has had great success in North America: "Love is not a feeling but a decision."

23. Remember the beautiful title of a book by Hans Urs von Balthasar, *Love Alone is Credible* (San Francisco: Ignatius Press, 2004). Love invites us to faith and justifies the act of faith.

Chapter 5 (pages 79–91)

1. Augustine, *On the Sermon on the Mount* I.1.1.

2. The majority opinion among biblical scholars is that Matthew and Luke, in redacting their gospels, shared two common sources: Mark's gospel for accounts of the events in the life of Jesus, and another source, known as "Q" for Jesus' discourses. Each of them also used written or oral traditions not used by the other.

3. Think of two strophes, of four Beatitudes each, which early Christians repeated orally.

4. There is a ninth Beatitude in the text of Matthew, but it is recognized that it repeats what is said in the eighth, "persecuted for justice," now specifically applied to the disciples of Jesus who are persecuted because they bear witness to their faith. The origin could be a supplication made by Jesus to his disciples at a moment when they were undergoing rejection by the crowds and persecution from religious authorities before the Passion.

5. Marcel Dumais, *Le Sermon sur la Montagne. État de la recherche, interprétation, bibliographie* (Paris: Letouzey et Ané, 1995), 331. I also published a smaller work intended to be accessible to a larger public: Marcel Dumais, *Le Sermon sur la montagne (Matthew 5–7)*, Cahiers Évangile 94 (Paris: Cerf, 1995), 76.

6. Three other texts proper to the Gospel of Matthew bear witness to the importance he gives to the theme of mercy and allow us to grasp its meaning: Matt 9:13; 12:7; and especially 23:23 (an anti-Beatitude).

7. In Matt 23:25-28, the scribes and the Pharisees are presented as the antithesis of the Beatitude of the pure of heart. They are called "hypocrites" because, for them, there is no correlation between what is inside and what is outside. They appear good but they are not. See also Matt 6:16-18. The "hypocrites" do religious actions (alms, prayer, and fasting) in order to be seen, not to please God. Since their motivation is false, their hearts are not pure.

8. Jesus does not say, "Blessed are those who are poor in spirit and meek . . . and merciful."

9. I was invited to present the Beatitudes to a group of young people. They are fascinated by the Beatitudes, especially when they are related to the life of Jesus. He was the first to live the Beatitudes he proclaimed.

10. Is not the attraction that Buddhism has in the West with "Christians who are baptized but not practicing" linked in attractiveness to the same values that Jesus proclaimed in the Beatitudes? The Dalai Lama has published two works in English on the way to happiness; both are best sellers.

11. Like the Sermon on the Mount in Matthew, the Sermon on the Plain in Luke, which also contains the Beatitudes, is addressed first to the disciples (Luke 6:20a), but it is also intended for the "great crowd" of people who had come to hear him (Luke 6:17-18; 7:1).

12. Evangelization thus has its goal: to receive God, the God of Love (the theological virtue), and to love one another (the moral virtue). This is what it means to "become fully human."

13. The Jewish author David Flusser, a specialist in New Testament times, has written: "The commandment to love one's enemies is so much his definitive characteristic that his are the only lips from which we hear the commandment in the whole of the New Testament"; See Flusser, *Jesus*, trans. Ronald Walls (New York: Herder & Herder, 1969), 70. P. Lapide, another contemporary Jewish author, shares this point of view.

14. This question and response should remain always with the evangelizing disciple and he or she will never finish responding. The response will always remain ultimately a response of faith, for even the supreme quality of the humanity of Jesus will not be a proof of his divinity.

Chapter 6 (pages 92–109)

1. Of the three stories recorded in chapter 24, the one about the disciples on the road to Emmaus not only occupies the central position, but it is also the most extensively developed: 23 verses out of 53 in the chapter.

2. The account has its parallel in the second volume of Luke, the Acts of the Apostles. Philip "evangelizes" the way Jesus does: first when he meets the Ethiopian on the road of his life. See Acts 8:26-39 and look for the parallel elements between this story and the one of Emmaus.

3. Jesus meets the disciples on their route of sadness and despair as he had encountered the Samaritan woman in the place of her thirst (John 4:1-26).

4. The beautiful pastoral constitution of the Second Vatican Council, "The Church in the Modern World" (*Gaudium et Spes*) begins with that admirable sentence, which indicates the route we should follow. See page 77.

5. Questioning as a teaching method is something that Jesus does frequently in the gospels. There are some 98 questions posed by Jesus in the gospels. In addition, the parables are questions of a sort.

6. Note that in v. 18 it is Cleopas who answers, but in v. 19 both travelers are involved in responding.

7. Listening carefully is an ascetical practice! It implies learning to be silent, not just waiting until the other person stops talking, but listening in such a way as to be able to hear and truly understand what is going on inside the other person and the significance of his or her personal experience. This is not self-evident, for it requires us to transcend ourselves, to get beyond our own ways of seeing things, of formulating and resolving problems, in order to enter into another's way of seeing things. On the other hand, it is a good opportunity to develop intellectual and psychological flexibility and to grow in humanity.

8. In fact, the disciples had only noticed predictions about the Messiah that they wanted to find in the Bible: the proclamation of a political kingdom and consequently an earthly messiah who would restore this kingdom. They were not open to another reading of the Scriptures that Jesus had already offered in and by his earthly life. This reading sees a kingdom that is at one and the same time interior (communion with God) and accomplished by fraternity among all human beings, where justice, help, and compassion have a predominant place. Such is the kingdom of God that Jesus inaugurated during his earthly life.

9. The Greek verb—very well translated by "stay with" or "remain" with them—is found frequently in the Gospel of Luke and likewise in the Gospel of John. Remember the well-known verse from the book of Revelation: "Behold, I stand at the door and knock. If anyone hears my voice and opens the door, I will enter his house and dine with him, and he with me" (Rev 3:20).

10. At the beginning of verse 30, Luke uses the same solemn formula that he had used at the beginning of verse 15 to introduce the initiative that Jesus took in encountering the two travelers on the road: "And it happened that" (*kai egheneto* in Greek). This signifies that what is going to happen will have an unsuspected meaning for them. In fact, the first action of Jesus prepares a second one. Jesus joins them on the road, but they do not recognize him. He does something with them at the table and they recognize him.

11. In the Gospel of Luke the four same verbs (took the bread, blessed it, broke it, and gave it) describe the actions of Jesus at two very significant moments: the multiplication of the loaves (Luke 9:16) and the Last Supper with his disciples (Luke 22:19). These four verbs are used in the church for the consecration of the bread and wine at eucharistic celebrations.

12. The sign of the divine is evanescent and transitory, like the transfiguration.

13. Two frequent situations: some who were baptized at birth have never really made a personal choice for faith and have stopped practicing the faith as society has been transformed from religious to secularized; others who were baptized have gradually drifted away from any relation with a God who was presented to them as a distant being or a judge.

14. Acts 9:2 and Acts 18:25-26. See also Acts 19:9; 19:23; 22:4; 24:14; 24:22. In India followers of Hinduism and Buddhism are often called "disciples of the Way."

15. The Greek verb used (*sudzètein*) describes a "heated discussion." This could indicate that they had differences of opinion.

16. The "heart" in the Scriptures does not designate the seat of feelings. It is the source of the most fundamental options in life.

17. Meditating on the account of creation in the first chapter of Genesis is a reminder concerning the temptation to fashion God in our image rather than letting ourselves be fashioned in his.

18. The Greek text says literally "And getting up." The Greek verb *anastantes* is also used to speak of the resurrection of Jesus. Thus, the two disciples are, as it were, "resurrected!" They have experienced a sort of resurrection that has put them back on their feet and set them out on the road toward the community of disciples.

19. In other words, when Jesus encounters persons who open themselves to his presence, he sends them on the way, establishes or reestablishes them in communion with the other disciples, and sends them forth as witnesses.

20. The affirmation, by the gathering of apostles and disciples, that the apostle Peter had encountered the Risen One (v. 34) precedes the account of the two disciples on the road, and, in a way, it confirms the truth of their story (v. 35).

21. In the parallel account of the encounter of Philip and the Ethiopian eunuch on the road to Gaza (Acts 8:26-40), the option for Jesus is expressed by the eunuch's reception of baptism, the first sacrament of faith.

22. At the beginning of their journey, the two travelers saw themselves as ex-disciples of a dead prophet; at the end they are disciples and witnesses of the living Lord.

23. If we are willing to listen to another, to dialogue with another, it needs to be done honestly. It requires willingness to receive from the other, even to change some of our perceptions. Not that we let go of our religious convictions, but perhaps we might be less absolute in our ways of speaking about them and our ways of expressing them in our lives. Nonetheless, we do have to evaluate just how far we can go in furthering the dialogue. Dialoguing about spiritual and religious questions presupposes that we clarify and deepen our own faith, and that we are willing to engage in a process of continuing formation in the faith. As witnesses, we have to know our limits and, at the proper moment, we should introduce those who ask us questions about our faith to individuals or groups who are more qualified than we are to answer their questions about spiritual and religious matters.

24. Joseph Bois, OMI, article in *Apostolat international* (March/April 2010), 29.

25. François Bovon, *Luke 3: A Commentary on the Gospel of Luke 19:28–24:53*, trans. James Crouch, Hermeneia—A Critical and Historical Commentary on the Bible (Minneapolis: Fortress, 2012), 370.

26. To the reasons here presented might be added the fact that the evangelist Luke likes to present a man and a woman side by side. See Luke 1:5-38 (Zacchary and Elizabeth) and Luke 15:3-10 ("What man among you with a hundred sheep . . . ? What woman with ten drachmas . . . ?).

27. There is no reason to assume that the women who accompanied Jesus and the Twelve—"and many others" according to Luke 8:3—were all widows. It is possible that couples also accompanied Jesus and the Twelve and "provided for them out of their own resources" (Luke 8:3).

Conclusion (pages 110–18)

1. The Word of the Gospel has a particular power that our human words do not have. The direct witness given by Jesus Christ in the gospels far surpasses the indirect word spoken by our limited and fragile life of a disciple on the way.

2. See also Acts 4:32-35; 5:12-16.

3. I know of dioceses where they have developed programs for those identified as "re-beginners." Obviously, new "converts and recently baptized" persons will be called to follow a course of Christian formation and catechesis, as in the primitive church (see Acts 2:42).

4. At the beginning of the third millennium two works by well-known authors appeared with evocative titles: Jean-Claude Guillebaud, *Le goût de l'avenir, Essai* [The Taste for the Future, an Essay] (Paris: Seuil, 2003), and Jean Vanier, *Made for Happiness: Discovering the Meaning of Life with Aristotle*, trans. Kathryn Spink (Toronto: House of Anansi, 2001). The original French title of the latter is *Le goût du Bonheur* (The Taste for Happiness).